leading

relationships

leading

relationships

build meaningful connections,

eliminate conflict, and

radically improve engagement

Steve McClatchy

WILEY

Published by John Wiley & Sons, Inc., Hoboken, New Jersey.
Published simultaneously in Canada.

For general information on our other products and services or for technical support, please contact
our Customer Care Department within the United States at (800) 762-2974, outside the United States
at (317) 572-3993 or fax (317) 572-4002.

Wiley also publishes its books in a variety of electronic formats. Some content that appears in print
may not be available in electronic formats. For more information about Wiley products, visit our web
site at www.wiley.com.

Library of Congress Cataloging-in-Publication Data Is Available:

ISBN 9781394289387 (Cloth)
ISBN 9781394289394 (ePub)
ISBN 9781394289400 (ePDF)

COVER DESIGN: PAUL MCCARTHY
SKY10093430_121224

This book is dedicated to my eleven brothers and sisters. Big families grow even bigger personalities. There isn't enough room on this page for how much you all mean to me. I just want to say once and for all that I was the best tennis player in the family. Now I will know who read this by who argues with me next time I see them.

Contents

Introduction

Leadership is a never-ending journey of continuous improvement. It's up to you as a leader to make sure your organization is continuously getting better and faster at serving the needs of your customers. To support that drive toward excellence, you need to build and maintain a company culture of respect and teamwork that encourages healthy relationships among colleagues, and fuels engagement, creativity, and innovation. In this atmosphere, your team can focus on creating quality products and services, instead of focusing on drama and games of ego and competition.

This book presents concepts and skills that leaders need in order to:

- Create and uphold company values so that every relationship can be functional and productive, and teams can focus on serving the customer.
- Identify and avoid toxic relationship games that can destroy company culture.
- Resolve and reduce employee conflicts.
- Hold people accountable for their agreements, including executing their job responsibilities in accordance with company values, without damaging the relationship.

- Make all business decisions with the best interest of the customer in mind.

- Build a business case for all opinion-based conversations and decisions.

- Highlight strengths and work around the weaknesses of the people on your team.

- Give positive and constructive feedback that improves the performance and productivity of the recipient, shows the recipient that you are a partner in their career, and confirms that you want them to be successful.

- Boost engagement, improve retention, and increase employees' job satisfaction.

- Build your company culture around the Five Levels of Maturity and remove toxic ego games from interactions across the organization.

- Meet the standards of behavior that can be expected from leaders who consistently work at Level Five Maturity.

Conflict and competition within teams are obstacles to productivity that cause turnover, drain resources, and get in the way of doing business. The concepts and skills in this book are the answer to these distractions. They are the building blocks of the healthy relationships you need to cultivate in your team so that you can more effectively serve your customers and lead toward continuous improvement in your business.

Why You Should Lead Your Relationships

More than anything else, business leaders want their business to be successful, which means customers choosing them over the competition, and delivering their products and services in a profitable way. Business leaders have to be continuously working on quality, speed, and reducing cost to create the greatest value for the customer, so that their product or service is chosen every time the customer has to make a purchasing decision. The most profitable way for a leader to spend their time is on the systems, processes, and structures that make their business better, faster, and more efficient, but a myriad of relationship-based issues get in the way of that focus. Communication problems, collaboration problems, turf wars, exclusionary alliances, conflict, people not meeting their obligations, tardiness, and absenteeism are all obstacles to running a business efficiently and focusing on serving the customer. These issues create relationship problems that

1

can drain company resources, including requiring the business leaders' attention and distracting them from customer-focused strategies.

As I rattle off these problem areas in my workshops, it seems like every head in the room is nodding along with me. Relationship problems create a complex environment that hinders teamwork, collaboration, innovation, creativity, concentration, and productivity. This gets in the way of doing business efficiently and focusing on the customer. This kind of dysfunctional company culture is often what leads clients to seek professional development consulting. When I ask clients why they are seeking professional development on this topic for their teams, classic answers sound something like this:

> *"We did an engagement survey that showed that our people are burned out and disengaged."*
>
> *"We're losing people. Our retention numbers are down, and the cost of acquiring new talent is rising."*
>
> *"We grew too fast and promoted people who weren't ready. They don't know how to lead or manage other people, and it's causing HR problems."*
>
> *"Our teams are spending more time arguing and talking behind each other's backs than producing content."*
>
> *"Ever since we hired this one team leader, that team has developed a toxic atmosphere, and they missed their last deadline."*

These are the kinds of symptoms that begin appearing when companies don't purposefully build a healthy workplace culture. As relationship problems develop, employees lose engagement with their work. In fact, Gallup's landmark Q12 Employee Engagement Survey[1] specifically revealed a direct correlation between the quality of an employee's relationships with their supervisor and colleagues and their level of engagement at work. This ultimately affects morale and retention in the organization.

The survey identified 12 employee needs that drive engagement, 10 of which directly relate to workplace culture. An organization's culture is a composite reflection of the amount of trust that is in every one-on-one relationship within that organization. Every relationship within a team has an effect on the team's culture and therefore on the engagement of every employee on that team. If businesses can address and improve relationship issues in their organization, they will increase engagement, improve morale, increase retention, and improve employee satisfaction, enabling teams to be more customer-focused and more effective.

Having good relationships with the people at work is the biggest contributing factor to satisfaction in the workplace. How much happier, more productive, more engaged, and more dedicated would employees be if relationships at work were smooth, respectful, and functional? Or even pleasant? Would they be happy to come to work every day? What would that do for company culture?

And it's not just about business relationships. What if they learned skills that made their personal relationships better also? What is it like to be in a personal relationship with you? In every relationship you have, what are you offering the other person? Are you rooting *for* them, or *against* them without realizing it? Do you tend to bring competition into conversations and relationships without meaning to? Do you subconsciously size yourself up against others in every situation? Do you have people in your life who do this? Do you find it to be emotionally draining? This spirit of competition and trying to win gets in the way of building healthy relationships and, as we will explore, gets in the way of doing business. Understanding this obstacle to success in relationships is the first step toward managing it so that we can focus on building fulfilling, mutually beneficial relationships in our personal lives and in business.

Good relationships don't just happen haphazardly without leading them in the right direction by setting a standard of behavior toward each other. Building trust, treating the other person with respect, encouraging the other's success, avoiding competition where it doesn't belong, honoring agreements, and highlighting the other's strengths are the skills needed to make relationships great. Leaders are tasked with mastering these skills so they can remove the issues that get in the way of building great relationships and doing business together.

The quality of our relationships is a determining factor in the quality of our life experience. If we can understand what is holding us back, improve what we bring to the table, and improve how we manage what the other person brings to the table, then we can improve *all* our relationships. In our personal life, this means an increase in happiness and quality of life because we relate better to the people who are important to us. In business this means avoiding office politics, games, drama, and conflict so that we can turn our focus back to the customer, driving revenue and results, and accomplishing the company's mission and goals.

CHAPTER

1

The Role of Relationships in Business

Good relationships are the foundation of our personal lives, but their place in business is less clear. Is it really necessary to build good relationships in business? An audience member approached me after a keynote speech and said, "These concepts are all great, but my company doesn't have a mission statement or company values. Relationships don't matter in our culture, so how am I supposed to fix any of these issues?"

My answer was that his company absolutely has a mission statement, although it may be unwritten. It's "make money." And the values of the company are "Anything that helps us make money is valued." This may sound funny or possibly distasteful to you, but I'm not making fun of them here. It's actually a valid default mission. All businesses exist for a reason – to make a profit. Even non-profit organizations need to raise more money than they spend, or else they will be ineffective in supporting their causes and unable to continue their charitable work. Many people have deeply rooted beliefs about money being evil or the pursuit of profit being evil, but businesses themselves are not capable of good or evil; they exist only to make a profit for their shareholders.

Sometimes I use the example that you aren't alive just to breathe, but if you can't breathe, you won't be alive for long. If a business doesn't make a profit for a prolonged period of time, it will cease to be in business. It will have to close. Then its employees will no longer have jobs to support their families. Its customers, who we hope benefited in a positive way from their products or services, will no longer benefit from them. Its vendors will lose a client and consequently lose revenue. Shareholders will lose their investments, which support their retirement. Its charities will no longer have a benefactor.

Basic economics teaches that one business closing can have a ripple effect proportionate to the size of that business in its market. The people involved in a business will suffer real consequences if it fails to make money. So, "make money" is the default mission underlying any additional expressed mission statement a company might have, because if it doesn't make money, it will have to close, and then that business and its stakeholders can't accomplish any additional mission statements either, no matter how meritorious those might be.

This fundamental truth of business raises some questions. If business is an atmosphere that exists to make money, where do relationships fit in? If we build great relationships, does that increase the company's revenue? Does it improve things like efficiency and productivity? Does the customer get a better experience when colleagues have better relationships? That may be difficult to quantify when everything is going well, but it starts to become clear when we can't get along. What if we make things difficult for each other, create a tense or even hostile work environment for the people around us, and don't trust each other? Is there a real cost to the business? Is getting along just a bonus thing that makes work more pleasant, or is there a real business impact from poor working relationships, even if the business does not espouse any values except making money? Does having good relationships really contribute to our ability to beat our competition, and be profitable, and accomplish our purpose as an organization, or is it just something that would be nice to have?

My Clients Have Already Answered These Questions for Me

I have a client in the food industry whose brand is fading. They're not where they were 20 years ago as a company, and they need to reinvigorate their brand. They need to innovate and streamline and find out how to become relevant to a new generation who doesn't have the experience with their brand that the previous generation did in a pre-global market with fewer players. They know what they must do, but they're having trouble getting it done because they can't agree on how to attack the problem. They've got employees who have been with the company for more than 30 years who have valuable perspectives, skills, and experience, and they've got young people whom they hired for their new ideas, energy, and potential, plus everyone in between. Now their multigenerational team members argue over strategy, misunderstandings, and disrespect. If they don't get their team unified toward reinventing their brand, they will be in danger of fading into oblivion.

At the same time, I have another client in the sports industry who is at the top of their market. They are experiencing an unprecedented surge in demand, sustainable growth challenges, and pressures to find the right talent among the swollen applicant pool. Everyone wants a piece of them right now. They have an incredible opportunity to capitalize on this popularity. They are on the brink of taking their business to new revenue heights, but the CEO just spent a whole afternoon dealing with HR issues because two of his senior executives in crucial departments don't get along, and they can't seem to get the next campaign off the ground. His time is so valuable right now, and instead of brainstorming ways to capitalize on their new "household-name" status, he has been defusing tension and policing petty arguments within his executive team. The opportunity in front of them won't last forever, and the CEO is very frustrated that his people aren't all hyper-focused on grasping it and doing whatever it takes to work together to keep the momentum going.

Another client of mine, with a popular niche clothing line, is frustrated because they have been missing repeated opportunities for growth. Their patriarch, who is no longer involved in the day-to-day operations, wanted it to be a small company but left them with debt to pay. The current executives, who are all related to each other, cannot agree whether to grow the company. Some want to honor the patriarch's vision for the company, but some see expansion as the only way to pay off debt and grow profits. Their disagreement and financial pressures threaten to disband the company altogether because the executives are guilting each other over their opinions.

Another client in the entertainment industry hired me to help reconfigure a top executive's role because she was knocking it out of the park as far as her department's revenues go, but her department had so much turnover that overhead was threatening the profit margin. She had trouble staffing her events because she was driving away good people right and left with her abrasiveness.

My government agency clients know they need to work on speed and quality in order to spend taxpayers' money more efficiently and effectively. What taxpayers want is for the government to provide services at the lowest cost and the best quality. Poor relationships in the office get in the way of that, increasing costs and impeding efficiency.

This Is Why Companies Should Care About Relationships

This is nothing new. I hear stories all the time about power plays among colleagues, hostile work environments, resignations tendered due to social issues at work, using job titles as a barometer for the validity of new ideas in meetings, withholding pertinent information to punish certain colleagues, purposely taking things out of context in order to embarrass others, and boardrooms taking sides in arguments regardless of the effect on the customer.

No, this is not sixth grade. These are real, educated adults with business experience. They are put in situations where they have to work closely with people they didn't choose. Without some preparation and guidelines, a lot can get in the way of these relationships being successful, and unsuccessful relationships within a company will get in the way of the company being successful. This is why companies should care about relationships. They are not going to attract and keep top talent and future leaders if the company culture is toxic. When I speak about this topic of relationships, everyone in the room usually has a story to share. Employees know when relationship issues are hindering their work or affecting how they feel when they go home at night.

First, Make Sure You Have the Capacity to Build Relationships

You can't work on business systems or address customer needs until you address the relationship problems that are in the way, yet you can't solve relationship problems when the people responsible for solving them are burned out. The feeling of burnout is a lack of excitement and improvement in your life when today looks just like yesterday and the day before, and nothing is happening today that will make tomorrow or even next year any better. When you're burned out, it affects how you treat people and affects your capacity for relationships with others. If I don't feel good about me, blaming you or criticizing you can make me feel better about me. If I don't have any progress or excitement in my life, I will find it difficult to cheer you on in yours. Unless I am in a good place, something good happening in your life will only make me feel worse about mine. Now instead of cheering for you in your marathon this weekend, I hope you trip. Instead of congratulating you on your job promotion, I am jealous and wonder why I haven't been promoted. Often the root cause of a relationship problem comes from either person not having the capacity for a relationship at all because they are burned out and not in a healthy place to be interacting with someone else, so they wind up mistreating the other person.

This is why personal leadership is important. My definition of leadership is improvement. Leadership should not be reserved for a few people at the top of the corporate power structure. Leadership is a choice you make, and in every situation there is an opportunity to lead. With this practical definition, anyone, in any situation, can be a leader regardless of their job position. Instead of being a title that you hold or a seat that you sit in, leadership is a result you produce by making something better than it was before. It requires vision of how your life, relationships, and business could be better in the future, and it requires purposeful actions today to bring about those changes in the future.

Personal leadership is a commitment to continuous improvement in some area of life.

Before you can lead your relationships in the right direction, you must practice personal leadership so that you have the capacity for relationships with others. Without it, the maintenance tasks in life can fill your days and weigh you down, leading to burnout. Personal leadership is leading, or improving, yourself by doing what you *don't* have to do every day: setting and pursuing goals that will improve your life and make tomorrow better than today.

Without a goal before you, life becomes stagnant. Tomorrow will look just like today and so will a year from now, and five years from now. The world around us is always changing and progressing in some way. If you aren't continuously progressing or improving something in your life, burnout will set in as you fight just to complete the daily maintenance of life. Pursuing continuous improvement and leading your life forward, instead of just managing whatever life throws at you, builds positive self-identity, which is the foundation of personal leadership, and which is necessary to build healthy relationships with others. A positive self-identity is what enables a leader to effectively lead others instead of competing with them out of jealousy or feeling threatened by their energy and accomplishments.

For more about this topic, see my book, *Decide: Work Smarter, Reduce Your Stress, and Lead by Example* (Wiley, 2014).

Once someone has committed to improvement in their lives and they build a positive self-identity based on that rather than sizing up against others, then they have the capacity for building great relationships with other people.

Leading relationships means encouraging, establishing, and supporting functional, respectful relationships among business colleagues, managers, employees, and clients so that we can build trust and confidence in the people around us, stop competing with each other, and focus on serving the needs of our customers. The same concepts and skills used to lead business relationships can help us purposefully lead (improve) our personal relationships too.

Good Relationships Are Crucial to Business Success

Think about your own personal experiences. Think of a time in your career when you had a difficult relationship with a colleague, boss, vendor, or client. What happened between you? What stories do you tell about working with that person? How do you feel when you hear their name? Have you heard other people tell stories like this about difficult people in their workplace? What emotions come through? Think of your own story or one you have heard from someone else. Listen and look for any impact on the business due to these two people not getting along. Does it impact productivity, creativity, engagement, morale of their teams, innovation, how ideas are generated and shared, the pace and rhythm of work in their teams, their speed in responding to customers, the quality of what gets produced, or the ability to share feedback? Did you have to double-check things, go through multiple approval or signature processes, and send everything in writing just to cover yourself?

- Think about *creativity*. Did you feel free to express ideas without fear of being criticized or of someone else taking credit?

- Think about *engagement*. Did you feel fully committed to the success of the project, or did you have a headache from eye-rolling so hard all day?

- Think about *innovation*. Did you feel free to suggest ways to improve processes without being accused of stepping on toes or being reminded of your subordinate place on the team?

- Think about *morale*. Did you feel that your contributions were appreciated? Did negative attitudes discourage collaboration?

- Think about *quality*. Did everything get done in the best possible way to serve the customer, or were you more concerned with internal issues? Did anyone skip a step in quality control because they didn't want to deal with a certain person?

- Think about *retention*. Did someone in these stories leave a job because a relationship became too difficult to endure? If so, the relationship cost that person a job and the time it took to find a new one. It also negatively impacted retention for that business.

- Think about *culture*. What if one of the people in that relationship was the aggressor and that person stayed behind in the company after driving out a good employee? Is there a risk of losing the next employee who works with that person, and the next, and the next? Is that company's culture now at risk because of one person?

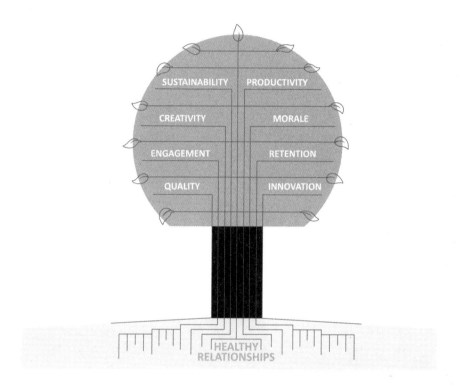

Have you heard stories like this? How much is it costing your business that people are not treating each other the way they want to be treated? How much is it costing your employees in terms of personal health and well-being? How much work interruption is the business experiencing because of turnover? Is there effective succession planning, including management training, so that the business can continue to move forward and thrive and learn from its past to create a stronger future? Or is there a scarcity mentality and efforts to keep people out of the "inner circle" at the top so that some people always know more than others and they get self-esteem out of that? Is there a collaborative environment, or is everyone reinventing the wheel all the time because no one wants someone else to prosper and be in a position to threaten their job? Is there is a supportive environment where people feel secure to share their ideas, or are you wasting the talent that you hired so that a top manager can retain control and feel empowered by that?

Work would be more enjoyable if everyone treated each other with respect. Studies show that people are much more willing to dedicate energy, effort, and mindfulness, and to work hard for their company if they have great relationships with their boss and colleagues. If the relationship isn't there, people are less likely to put in the extra effort it would take for the work process to succeed. The pace of business slows down when relationships are failing. If you don't insist on and maintain a safe, healthy work environment for your employees to collaborate, share ideas, and work comfortably with each other, then it will cost your company money through lost retention, less innovation, and lower market share among other ways. That has been proven.[1]

> If your organization values the health and well-being of its employees, then learning skills like conflict resolution, communicating effectively, and building trust is a no-brainer.

Even if your company's only mission statement is "make money," don't just think about relationship issues as *Wouldn't it be nice? We would all be happier if we could just get along.* You can connect these relationship issues directly to the bottom line of the organization just by listening to the stories of difficult relationships and how they resulted in shattered metrics for the business.

The High Cost of Low Trust

Research data reveals that the turnover of just one mid-level employee can be a significant cost to a small company. In fact, replacing an employee costs on average 50–60% of the annual salary for that position.[2] Turnover is not the only expensive result of workplace conflicts. Add lost productivity, increased sick days, increased medical claims, and legal costs attributed to workplace conflict for an estimated grand total cost of $200 billion per year to the US economy.[3] That staggering figure proves that relationship issues are important to people, as if we needed hard data to know that. According to an annual employee satisfaction survey, "Relationship with Supervisor" consistently ranks as one of the most important elements leading to job satisfaction.[4] Another recent survey revealed that more than 60 million US workers are dealing with workplace bullying, described as abuse, humiliation, or intimidation interfering with job performance.[5] In the opening paragraphs to both of these studies, the problems are described as "unavoidable" and "global."

Relationship issues affect our day-to-day workplaces as much as they affect our personal lives because we deal with real people in both settings. We have the same feelings and sensitivities at work as we do outside of work. People involved in workplace conflicts can experience a range of effects, including anxiety, depression, exploitation, anger, frustration, stress, helplessness, disengagement, and burnout. Once they are in that state, their personal relationships are usually affected, and then those suffer as well, compounding the effects on a worker's life. Especially with more people working remotely and able to work anytime, anywhere, there is even more transference of workplace stress into a worker's home life.

The Health of Our Relationships Has Real Physiological Effects

Studies clearly show that negative social interactions cause negative physiological effects on the body, and positive social interactions have positive physiological effects on the body.

Negative workplace interactions, poor relationships at work, and a company culture that does not uphold respect for others are significant sources of workplace stress. Stress causes complex physiological responses in the body, which can lead to chronic health issues, including medical, psychological, and behavioral problems, and is a major cause of workplace absenteeism. The impact of long-term stress on the body has been linked to cardiovascular disease, cancer, and increased risk of physical injuries. Anxiety and depression have also been linked to stress, and depression is a significant factor in illness and disease, as well as a loss of productivity in the workplace. The instance of substance abuse (including alcohol, tobacco, and prescription drug abuse) is directly correlated to increased stress, and is a major contributing factor to work absenteeism, lost productivity, and increased incidences of workplace aggression and on-the-job accidents.[6] One study even found that feeling ostracized or isolated in the workplace has the same effect on the brain as experiencing physical pain.[7]

The opposite of this is also true. Just as negative relationship interactions can cause negative physiological results, positive close relationships can help reinforce biological systems that promote physical healing and release happiness hormones, triggering satisfaction and joy. One study found that in response to positive social interactions the brain produced a powerful painkiller that sparks trustworthiness and motivation to help others.[8]

These studies report that our brains process positive and negative relationship experiences just as they process physical pain and painkillers.[9] The effects of these interactions follow suit. Just as negative interactions cause physical and psychological problems, positive interactions can boost the body's natural ability to combat stress and build cardiovascular strength.

Employees with positive workplace relationships are not only healthier, but they are also more engaged, report higher job satisfaction, are more likely to stay in their jobs longer, have better concentration, and feel free to think more creatively.

Good Relationships Are Vital to an Organization Accomplishing Their Work

All this research proves that poor relationships, workplace conflicts, and an atmosphere of low trust result in real costs to businesses. These issues affect the speed, quality, efficiency, and cost of your work, which means they are integral to your company's ability to complete their mission, how well it can be completed, and how cost-effectively it can be completed.

Are efficiency and profit the only goals? Of course not. We all want our work to be meaningful, fulfilling, and appreciated. Having good working relationships and removing unnecessary drama, hostility, tension, or even just constant misunderstandings in our workplaces can help us to reduce stress and approach work with the freedom to offer creative and innovative ideas without fear of ridicule or unfair criticism. This creates the pleasant working environment that employees deserve. That's the atmosphere that will help companies succeed, and that's the reason that smart companies promote values like respect and teamwork instead of just "make money." They know that financial success is only possible when people are working together, instead of against each other, and they know that people can rarely have long-term success working together in an environment that ignores relationship issues.

CHAPTER

2

What Builds Great Relationships?

Good relationships are built with trust, and trust is rooted in action. I can't just tell you to trust me; you have to observe my actions and habits to see for yourself if you can trust me. We have to consistently act reasonably and respectfully toward each other to establish trust so that we can successfully do business together, educate together, govern together, or live together. If we work together and you don't trust me, you will subconsciously be focused on always protecting yourself in our interactions, instead of being fully engaged in the task at hand. For the purpose of this book, let's define trust.

Trusting you completely means I have unwavering confidence that you will always act in my best interest.

When I give this definition, many people ask, "What if we're both applying for the same job? If I always work in your best interest, then wouldn't I want you to get the job and not me? But I'm applying for it too, so isn't that mutually exclusive?" My answer is no, it's not. We both should want the person who is most qualified to get the job. It would not be in your best interest to get a job if you are not the most qualified person for the job, and you shouldn't want that for me either if you're acting in my best interest. My employees and peers in that new job would not respond well to me as a leader knowing that someone *let* me get the promotion versus them when they were more qualified. That situation causes stress, regret, and most likely leads to resignation or termination. If you act in my best interest, you want me to get the job that I am the best person to fill, then I can thrive professionally and have the personal capacity for healthy relationships.

Sometimes people ask, "Who goes first?" as in "I'll act in your best interest if you act in mine." That's simple. A leader goes first. Even in peer-to-peer relationships there is an opportunity to lead the relationship. If you act in the other person's best interest and show them that they can trust you, even if they haven't done it first, you are leading the relationship in the direction of trust. If they meet you there, then you know you can trust them in return.

If trusting someone depends on their actions, then we can identify what actions establish (or maintain) trust, increase trust, and destroy trust.

What Actions Establish, Increase, and Destroy Trust?

If we work to develop a basic level of trust with everyone, we interact with on a regular basis, our communication and interactions with them will be smoother, more effective, more efficient, and more pleasant. The easiest way to establish a basic level of trust in a relationship is to always do what you said you would do.

> Trust is established or maintained in a relationship when you do what you said you would do.

Every time someone shows up when they say they will, calls you back when you ask them to, or delivers on their project piece when they were supposed to, it shows us we can trust them, or continue to trust them. Doing what we said we would do is what is expected of us as adults. This is relationship *management* (or maintenance). It keeps the relationship going so that trust does not erode. It's being reactive by complying with "have-to" requests and preventing the consequences in the relationship that might arise if we don't do what we said we would do.

While simply maintaining trust by doing what we said we would do is not exactly *leading* the relationship, it is necessary in order to keep your relationships intact and alive, and relationships can continue to function well this way, support productivity at work, and not cause relationship problems. Doing what you said you would do includes completing tasks and workflow according to company values, which means attitude counts. Every organization should value treating each other with respect. Interaction between team members should be free of drama, games, power plays, and hostility to ensure a healthy and pleasant environment for everyone.

Although this sounds simple, it doesn't go without saying, and many people find it challenging to simply do what they said they would do. However, if you want someone to trust you, you must act in their best interest by doing what you said you would do.

> Trust is increased in a relationship when you do something you didn't have to do for the other person's best interest.

Trust in a relationship increases to a new level when you go above and beyond what is expected and you do something you didn't have to do that is in the other person's best interest. If I'm going out to grab lunch and I pick up something for you also, even when you didn't ask me to, it shows you that I'm thinking of you when you aren't around, and I have your best interest in mind. If I send you a text with a funny story or a good article or if I initiate a chance to work together or socialize together, it shows you that I'm reaching out and investing in our relationship. If I provide help without being asked or see a need that you have and I try to address it, that builds trust. If I see an injustice you're subjected to and speak out for you, if I compliment the work you're doing and ask questions so I can learn from it, recommend you as an expert in your field, or speak highly of you when you aren't around, those things increase the level of trust you have in me.

Doing something you don't have to do improves the relationship and takes it from where it was to a higher level of trust. This is leadership in relationships. It's being proactive in relationships rather than reactive. Have you ever gone to a party and the host had your favorite beverage for you? Or has someone texted you a picture while they were on vacation or brought you back a souvenir from their trip? When someone does something they didn't have to do for you, they're saying, "I want to have a better, stronger relationship with you," or "I was thinking about you when you weren't around." We recognize desire in their actions because if they did something they didn't *have to* do, why did they do it? It was something they *wanted* to do. It's over and above what is expected.

When someone does more than what is expected from them in their job, we say they are *passionate* about their job. They are driven by a desire for greater results because they love their job, and they care about the quality of what they produce. If you're doing something you don't have to do, whether it's for a career, hobby, or philanthropic cause, then you're demonstrating desire and passion for it. That's also what we want to see in our important relationships. We want to see desire; we don't want it to be only transactional or imposed by expectations.

This is how we've made friends, it's how we've found partners, it's how our kids know we love them. If you're going above and beyond the minimum by thinking about me when I'm not around, doing something I didn't expect, filling a need that I have without me asking you to, offering a nice gesture to let me know you care about me, demonstrating a desire to take our friendship or partnership to the next level of trust, and then I reciprocate, then we can have a great relationship. This is how we learn to trust, and it's how our family, best friends, most trusted partners, and people we trust the most in the world became close to us.

We can't approach every relationship we have in this way. It would be exhausting and probably insincere and possibly not even welcomed by some people. Our best relationships are the ones we have cultivated this way, over time, with both people making investments in the relationship on a similar, if not equal, level. These are relationships we are passionate about, and we are willing to do more than the minimum required, more than what's expected, to make them great. We aren't just checking off the minimum boxes in the relationship like returning the other person's calls or texts or saying hello when we see them. Those things are just common courtesy and basic respectful behavior. Obviously, we expect more than that from our best relationships. We are aware of and are invested in the other person's needs, moods, responsiveness, opinions, and wellness. If there is a relationship we are passionate about, we can deepen trust by doing more than the minimum expected and investing in the relationship.

Trust is damaged when someone doesn't do what they said they would do.

Each time someone falls short of doing what they said they would do, or acts contrary to our best interest, our trust in them erodes a little. If these actions continue, or if the actions are severe, our trust in them can be destroyed.

Whether it's not showing up for a planned social event, being late for a meetup, divulging a secret, or a betrayal of a more serious nature, each time someone doesn't do what they said they would do, it erodes a little of our trust. Everyone has that friend who likes to leave their options open for a weekend, takes a better offer at the last minute, or ignores your communications occasionally. They like to be known as spontaneous and exciting.

But when we need a reliable friend, we know that is someone we can't count on. Perhaps that's the reason they do it – they don't want the responsibility of people depending on them.

People who handle relationships this way in their personal lives often find it especially difficult to navigate relationships in business. Not showing up for a meeting, being chronically late, not submitting work on time, letting a team down on their part of a project, ghosting vendors and colleagues instead of handling problems, and making excuses for everything can all affect their career success. Being unreliable and untrustworthy in business often has serious consequences, such as not being chosen for a team, a project, or a promotion, or even being fired. In our personal lives, these things can affect our level of confidence and intimacy in the friendship. If I don't trust someone to do what they said they would do, I find it difficult to get too close to them or spend a lot of time with them.

What Is It Like to Work in a Low-Trust Environment?

If we don't trust someone or we have conflict with someone at work, then the atmosphere is ripe for games to ensue, usually in a passive-aggressive manner. Delayed communication, delayed workflow, territory wars, gossip, rejecting the chain of authority, and personnel turnover are among the ways that my clients have reported relationship issues compromising the success or quality of their projects, products, and services. Here are just a few examples of situations my clients have encountered because of a low-trust environment. In all of these scenarios, think about where the customer's experience is being prioritized.

- Donna emailed Mike with a question, but Mike wasn't able to get the info to answer the question for two days, so the next time Mike emailed Donna, Donna waited two days to respond even though she was available, and she already had the information needed to respond. She was simply retaliating for the delay. When she was called out for it, Donna blamed technology for ghosting Mike, saying his message went into her spam folder at first.

- Louis knew a proposal was due the next day, but he left at 4:30, telling his coworkers that his boss, Jeff, is always condescending to him so Jeff can stay late and fend for himself on the proposal.

- Jessica had an idea for a way to cut production costs but the person next to her at the meeting had a bad attitude and was grunting under his breath at everything that was being discussed. Jessica did not want to get shot down publicly so she kept her mouth shut and refused to share her idea for weeks until there was a more private meeting.

- Rachel was out on vacation for a four-day weekend and her client needed something. Sheila chose to ignore the client and not help out by just saying it would have to wait until Rachel returned because Sheila was jealous that Rachel was on vacation. Sheila hadn't taken any vacation days all year so Sheila thought Rachel's account should suffer because of her absence.

- Everyone at one company knew that the real exchange of information would take place in the hallway *after* the official meeting, when a certain exclusive group including a senior manager and her friends would say what they were *actually* thinking during the meeting instead of sharing it with the group. This meant that team members could never be sure they all had the same information and were going to approach the project with a unified plan, so the meeting was just wasted time for everyone because they didn't trust that the outcomes that were agreed upon would actually be put into place.

- Alex had to wait for Tom to complete his part of a project in order to work on the next part, but he observed Tom dawdling and doing other nonurgent things. He accused Tom of purposely holding up his part of the project in order to give Alex less time to work on his part. The supervisor admitted to me that Alex was probably right about Tom's motives being passive-aggressive, but there was no way to prove that so he couldn't do anything about it.

- Dana was put in charge of a project that Katrina thought should have been given to her. Katrina is now on Dana's team. Dana went over the details of the deliverables with her team, and Katrina said she agreed with her results. When Dana presented the results in a general meeting, Katrina spoke up and listed reasons, which were clearly prepared in advance, why her results were faulty.

- Robert reports that his sales team has dropped to about 60% of last year's revenue because the new sales manager is getting in the way of every sale. The new manager is young and feels that he needs to impose a powerful and controlling presence, so he is requiring unnecessary updates, holding lengthy meetings asking about the status of each stage of the sales cycle, and since they have not hit their numbers, he has just implemented an expense freeze, which further restricts access to clients. He does not welcome feedback about his methods, and salespeople are starting to leave due to the frustration of being micromanaged and the reduced earning potential.

- Samantha is used to being praised for her good ideas. When Daniel was brought in from a different department and presented challenges to one of her ideas along with an alternative, she not only shot it down publicly but asserted her dominance in the office by announcing to Daniel that everyone in the room agreed with her. Eye rolls and shocked expressions from the room indicated that she had not asked everyone if they actually agreed, but no one was brave enough to speak up due to her management position.

It may sound unattainable but shouldn't we, at a minimum, be able to expect civil, respectful, reasonable behavior from people? The answer is yes, we *should* be able to expect that, but we will not always get it.

These petty behaviors in everyday business situations are more common than you probably think. A recent think tank study[1] revealed that 44% of respondents admitted to seeking revenge at work for a range of scenarios, from serious offenses like taking credit for someone's else's ideas and abuses of power, to petty offenses like eating someone's lunch. The forms of revenge had a similar range of malicious intent with mild to serious consequences, like spreading rumors, tampering with someone's work equipment, and getting them fired.

Does it sound like these employees are focused on the client? On product quality? On profit margin? No. They are focused on getting even, or perhaps inflating their own self-image by tearing down someone else, or at least they are focused on what is going on internally with their colleagues, not on the client's experience. Just for a minute, pretend you are the business owner. How angry does this scenario make you? While these two employees are arguing and being passive-aggressive and having their feud, who is looking after the customer? Who is getting the work done on time? Who is protecting our reputation with the customer? Who is being cost-conscious? Are you babysitting here? This is costing you time and money, and worse yet, it could cost you a client. One or both of them has to go.

> When employees take their eye off the customer and turn their eye toward each other, the customer loses.

If the customer loses consistently, the business will eventually lose to their competition. This is how low trust and conflict affect a company's ability to thrive, and this is why high-trust functional relationships are important to business.

3

What Gets in the Way of Building Great Relationships?

From reading my clients' stories in the previous chapter, it's easy to see how relationship problems get in the way of doing business. But what gets in the way of great relationships? If we know which actions build, maintain, and destroy trust in relationships, why don't we build trust more consistently? Why don't we go out of our way for people? Why don't we do more than the minimum for the people in our lives? Why don't we strive to make all of our relationships great?

The Ego Is Your Best Survival Tool and Your Biggest Obstacle

The biggest obstacle people face in building great relationships in business and in their personal life is the same. It all starts with the ego. Not the negative connotation of inflated self-worth and conceit that we have when we hear the word "ego," but the ego everyone has as a sense of self-identity, self-esteem, and self-worth. It's a part of everyone. We can't just get rid of it and proceed without one. It has to be managed and controlled, directed, and respected, or else relationship problems will follow. If someone said to you, "Hey, can we talk about your ego?" you probably wouldn't think a compliment is coming your way. In fact, your ego would probably trigger a defensive reaction immediately. The concept of ego has a poor reputation in most circles outside the psychology journals. How did this vital and very personal part of the human psyche that forms our self-image get commonly reduced to an overbearing and annoying personality trait?

The ego is the spirit of self-preservation and positive self-worth that makes us believe we are worthy of survival.

It's because the ego has an important job to do, and it tends to put in a lot of overtime. In our inexhaustible built-in drive for survival, we have to believe that we are *worthy* of survival and of favorable things happening to us. That positive self-worth comes from the ego. The ego's job is to assert our needs in any situation and to get our needs met. It helps us thrive by driving us to survive and succeed. It's that little voice inside you that roots you on, backs you up, supports your choices, wants affirmation, seeks attention and approval, and is frequently trying to figure out a way for you to be right. It's bolstered by compliments, accolades, and likes on social media. It helps you have the confidence to apply to a college, apply for a job, give a speech, find a partner, try a new skill, or anything that takes courage and confidence. Without a healthy sense of self or ego, these things would be insurmountable. It's why we want to put only our best life on social media and assert a positive image to the world, and it's all about winning in any win-lose situation.

Your ego wants to differentiate you from the people around you. Its job is to make you feel unique and special, to feel valued for creating something, contributing to something, excelling at something, or making progress toward something. If you are leading your life toward continuous improvement by pursuing your goals and passions, instead of just getting burned out doing the daily grind, you will build a positive self-identity and a healthy ego, and you will develop a unique sense of who you are because of it. When you are thriving in this way, your ego is satisfied, and you are unthreatened by someone else who is happy or successful at something, because you yourself are seeking improvement. That kind of personal leadership is what keeps your ego satisfied. Without that forward motion, your energy is spent on all your daily responsibilities, and you start to feel like you have no choices. Then what will the ego's insatiable need for survival among your peers drive you to do?

A healthy response to being stuck in this rut would be that you might just feel bad enough about your current situation to make some big changes in your life toward improvement. This would be hard work, and you may have to fight your own ego to be this reflective and face tough truths enough to turn your situation around. For example, if you were to honestly answer why you feel threatened by someone else's success, would the honest, reflective answer be one of the following?

- "I'm not living up to my potential at work."
- "I should have been in a management role by now. What have I been missing?"
- "I've watched way too much TV recently. I need to get back into real life."
- "I've been spending above my means, and I need to reel it in."
- "I've been thinking about opening that side business for years and haven't done anything about it, and now I feel stuck. I think it's time."
- "I've been avoiding that situation for months, and I need to face it so I can put it behind me."
- "I've been doing nothing this year but work and paying bills. I'm so burned out, and I have nothing to look forward to."

This is using the competitive spirit of the ego toward yourself to propel you forward and work on improving your life. It requires things like honesty, determination, patience, and humility.

Unfortunately, here is what usually happens instead. The lazier and more common response that many people take is that they will turn the competitive spirit of the ego outward and try to compensate for feeling bad about their current situation by comparing themselves to others and finding a way to feel superior, thereby covering up any uncomfortable self-doubts with criticism of other people. They are grading their life on a curve compared to others, instead of striving for excellence themselves.

This type of jealous reaction can spark petty behavior like starting rumors or spewing tedious criticism. These negative thoughts and words about others make them feel better about themselves without actually having to change or accomplish anything.

When people are burned out or unhappy, they will get their self-identity from competing and sizing up against other people and making themselves feel superior in some way. This is where many relationship problems begin.

This instinctive response to size up against others when we feel dissatisfied is comparable to the instinctive fight-or-flight response to a survival threat. It's like evaluating a threat from a predator. If early man felt vulnerable because he was in a weakened state and a predator was near, he would evaluate both his ability to win a fight and his ability to flee, and he would instinctively decide which response gave him the greater likelihood of survival. When you are burned out or stuck in a rut and you measure up against the people you interact with, even subconsciously, the competitive spirit of the ego will drive you to determine that your greatest likelihood of survival is if you are stronger than your peers in some way. When we are unhappy and we hear of someone else's success or aptitude at something, it can trigger this instinctive response, and we look for a way to feel superior or stronger than they are by finding fault with them in some way. It's a defensive act of self-preservation.

This temporary feeling of empowerment does not fix the root problem. People who tend to react this way to other people's success in order to lift themselves up will have to do this again and again because it doesn't make their underlying dissatisfaction go away. It makes them critical of others, but it doesn't make them content with themselves.

I bet you know someone who has a habit of doing this. They can turn any conversation into a competition. They can one-up you in any category, and they always try to win by beating you at something or talking louder or faster than you to tell their stories. That's the displacement of the ego. That's the ego wanting to win in a situation where winning and losing is not appropriate. Their drive to compete and win comes from a lack of self-identity and a lack of satisfaction with their lives, from not knowing what makes them unique and special. They've identified something in you that they want to beat, but they don't understand how, and maybe they don't even understand why. If they're not feeling good about themselves, they might not only compete with you but might even root against you by talking behind your back, or worse. And perhaps they interact with *everyone* they meet in this way, not just you. My clients frequently tell stories of ego-driven problems at work, from petty behavior like excluding someone from group lunches or starting a rumor, to even sabotaging someone's work or computer. For some people, this simply becomes a habit of how they deal with disappointment, rejection of their ideas, constructive criticism, perceived threats to their position in a work or social group, or any other negative vibes from strangers, friends, coworkers, neighbors, even family. This is the ego taking over in place of reason and good judgment and going for the win.

To our primal brain, winning means survival; it means a successful hunt or escaping a predator. Failure, or losing, at these tasks means *not* surviving. The first job of your ego is to give you the drive to stay alive, or the survival instinct. If you make a bad decision concerning your happiness, you have tomorrow to try to be happy again, but if you blow a survival decision, there is no tomorrow. This unquenchable survival instinct even drives desires like looking your best, performing at your best, being proud of your accomplishments, seeking justice, demanding equality, negotiating a fair deal, and avoiding things that aren't in your best interest. The survival instinct of the ego is hard at work in a competitive environment.

From a young age our experiences train us to expect competition as a normal backdrop of life, whether it be healthy or unhealthy. In school, class rankings put you in competition with your classmates. In the school play, you might get the lead role . . . or you might be cast as "sheep #4." Sports are obviously competitive by nature. On the playground or in gym class, who is picked first and last for teams? In high school and college, there are popularity contests, whether stated or unstated. Then we grow up and get into business, and it's where do you work, what's your title, what car do you drive, what neighborhood do you live in, where do your kids go to school, and does your office have a window? We may not purposely seek competition in these areas, but the opportunity for competition is there if we look for it. The ego seeks to protect us in these situations. When it comes to any win-lose competition, your ego is your best asset, and it often kicks into overdrive to prevent you from losing.

Despite this wingman capability, when you hear the word *ego* in general conversation, it has a mostly negative connotation. You're never going to hear *Oh, she has a great ego!* If people are talking about someone's ego, it's almost certainly a problem. That's because, aside from a therapist or maybe a parent, other people don't evaluate us favorably on how well we assert our own needs and get them met in any given situation. If your ego is working fervently and assertively to win, one aspect of life where that will certainly work against you is in your relationships.

Relationships don't work on a win-lose basis. Bringing winning and losing into relationships will very likely destroy them because they work on a different premise than win-lose.

The success of relationships is governed by people's needs. Relationships work only when *both* people get their needs met.

If someone is winning and someone is losing, that means only one of them is getting their needs met and the other isn't, and then the relationship can't thrive, and possibly can't even survive. If you ever won or lost in a relationship, then you probably no longer have that relationship.

Relationships Have to Meet the Needs of Both Parties

Let's look at examples of needs in a few different types of relationships. A simple relationship with few needs is between you and your favorite restaurant. What you need is good food, good service, a clean environment, a good atmosphere, and a fair price. When those needs are met, you will probably return to that restaurant, which in turn satisfies their need for paying customers who will speak favorably about their restaurant and will return. After a bad experience in one of these categories, you probably wouldn't return or recommend that restaurant to your friends. You might even post a bad review, which impacts their ability to grow their business. If that happens with enough customers, the restaurant will go out of business. The relationship works only if both of you get your needs met. If one of you does not, the relationship will end.

To add some complexity, let's examine the relationship you have with your employer. Think of all the needs in your life that you are able to meet because you have a job. If you have ever been unemployed for a period of time, then you truly understand how many needs your job meets for you. It surely covers anything that involves money, including the monumental need to provide for your family, but that's only one of the 18 needs listed on my Employment Motivation Checklist (see Figure 3.1). Most often, people rank other needs higher than salary on the checklist. The most highly ranked needs among my workshop

EMPLOYMENT MOTIVATION CHECKLIST

To discover your number one employment motivator, rank each of the following 18 items. Pick your number one answer from each group of six and from your top three select your overall number one.

Job security ___

Interesting work ___

Growth/Development/Gain experience ___

Enjoy the day-to-day tasks of the job ___

Freedom/Autonomy/Empowerment ___

Overall benefits package ___

Promotions/Advancement ___

Relationships with coworkers ___

Belief in mission, purpose, or impact of organization ___

Fair and consistent work environment ___

Social aspects of work environment ___

Company (brand, size, locations, success, growth) ___

Relationship with supervisor or manager ___

Recognition and appreciation ___

Belonging/Being part of something bigger ___

Commute/Work from home options/Travel ___

Hours/Flexibility of schedule/Vacation/PTO ___

Pay/Bonuses/Raises/Ownership/Stock ___

Ask your supervisor to complete the checklist with respect to their own perceptions of what motivates you, and then share your responses. Discuss similarities & differences.

FIGURE 3.1 I use this Employment Motivation Checklist in my workshops to inspire attendees to think about what is most important to them in their current role.

Image courtesy of Alleer Keynotes & Workshops.

participants are Relationship with supervisor or manager, Relationships with coworkers, Freedom/Autonomy/Empowerment, Interesting work, Growth/Development/Gain experience, and Enjoy the day-to-day tasks of the job.

That's a lot of needs that we expect our jobs to meet for us. Now think of all the needs that you are meeting for the organization, all the work you do, all the emails you handle, all the questions you answer, and all the problems you solve. This relationship works only if both you *and* your employer are getting your needs met. If you are not making enough money to meet your needs or the atmosphere at work is toxic or unhealthy, then it isn't working for you. If your employer is not benefiting enough from the work that you do to justify your salary, then it isn't working for them. Some people start a job and leave after three months; some people start a job and stay for their whole career. We each decide: *what are my needs that this relationship must meet, and what am I willing to sacrifice in order to have these needs met?* The principle that both sides must get their needs met in order for it to succeed governs the success of the relationship. This takes the emotion out of any business relationship, whether it's employer-employee, client-vendor, or another similar relationship. If one side is no longer meeting the other side's needs, then the relationship is no longer a good fit.

This principle is vital to personal relationships as well. You have important needs of friendship, family, or partnership that you are trying to meet through relationships with the people in your life. Each of these relationships will only work if both you and the other person are meeting each other's needs. If one or both of you are pursuing needs that are mutually exclusive to the other person's needs, then the relationship will be troubled, to say the least, if not toxic. Balancing this usually requires prioritizing needs so that both people are satisfied.

This seems like such a simple principle, until you add the egos of the two people involved. If someone is competing in a relationship and trying to *win* in order to feel good about themselves, then they are trying to make the other person *lose*, even if they don't realize it. It could be an unintended consequence, but that doesn't change the reality that if someone wins, then someone loses. This is where relationships have trouble, and it's where the ego gets a bad name. When two people should be trying to meet each other's needs, there's no room for competition. People who bring winning and losing into everything don't understand this. If someone is competing in order to build their self-esteem, they can't meet the other person's needs in that mindset. In their quest for a positive self-identity, they have let the competitive spirit of the ego take over the relationship because it's easier to size up against others than to point that competitive spirit toward themselves and work on improving and balancing their life in order to build that positive self-identity in a healthy way.

Games and Competition

Games are supposed to have competition; it's in their nature, and playing games is how we're supposed to learn good sportsmanship because someone wins and someone loses – that's how games work. If you play checkers with someone, you expect them to try to win the game, but then after the game you expect good sportsmanship; you don't expect them to think they won at being a better person than you are because they beat you at checkers. That's healthy competition.

We all know it doesn't always work that way. Everyone has experienced a poor sport, whether it's on the playground or at higher-level sports, card games, board games, class rank, job offers, or business deals. We see it in professional sports and politics too often. There are plenty of people who get too involved, and they think their win or loss at a game or competition of some kind defines who they are as a person or somehow determines their worth. They do not understand (or they can't control) their competitive spirit.

On the other hand, and sometimes *because* of those overly aggressive people, there are many who think that *all* competition is unhealthy and should be eliminated, even in sports. This is the "we don't keep score" and "everyone gets a trophy" phenomenon that has gained popularity in kids' sports leagues. But healthy competition actually does belong in sports so that kids can learn how it feels to be rewarded for working hard at something and learn how to win and lose with dignity, compassion, honor, and decency. Teaching good sportsmanship in both winning and losing is necessary for healthy development and training in how to deal with both disappointment and success in life, as well as dealing fairly and respectfully with other people. It's also an exercise in being kind, showing support for friends, knowing your worth, and in having pride balanced with humility.

We should use these opportunities to teach children (and adults) that just because someone won or lost in a game doesn't mean they're better than the other team at being people. Whoever decided that competition in kids' sports should be eliminated probably had good intentions, perhaps something like this: *We don't want competition to enter into the kids' relationships, so if we take the score out of everything, there's no confusion between winning and having great friendships.* They disdain score-keeping because they have seen people who take advantage of that and keep score in relationships, and then they can't separate that from scorekeeping where it's appropriate. They try to control the situation by avoiding it, instead of teaching the important concept of good sportsmanship and of keeping competition where it belongs.

A game is about keeping score, but that means someone loses; that's how games work. When we play games of win-lose in a relationship and the ego takes over instead of meeting the other person's needs, it becomes difficult for the other person to want to continue to meet our needs, and the relationship has begun to fall apart. Whether you see yourself as the winner or the loser in the relationship, you will no longer be focused on meeting each other's needs; you will be focused on the competition, and on how it has affected you. This erodes the trust that two people need to have in order to be successful in any relationship, whether it be personal or professional.

Putting this concept into practice in business means that if I see a new colleague on their first day at the company, I should probably welcome them and say something like "Hi, I'm Steve, welcome to the organization. If I can be a resource to you, please reach out to me. I hope you have a long and successful career here. I'll be in the breakroom for lunch today if you'd like to join me." I should be thinking of how I would like to be welcomed if it were my first day and I knew no one, then I should try to meet the new colleague's needs of acceptance, kindness, and respect. However, the competitive factor of the ego gives us a little pause before we introduce ourselves to someone; it prevents us from initiating relationships, being vulnerable, and going first. It stops us from saying *"I'll work in your best interest even though I'm not sure if you will work in mine."*

The ego and its win-lose inclination does not want us to take those risks. My ego might stop me from introducing myself and making myself vulnerable to you like that because I don't trust that you will respond in the same way. You might try to win, and then I would lose. So instead of trying to meet your needs, I am thinking about competition and whether you might try to establish dominance in the relationship, and now I will walk right by you instead of acknowledging you and giving you a chance to reject me.

In situations like this, if people are insecure, the ego might prompt them to protect themselves and they might respond by feigning lack of interest, bravado, or superiority in order to conceal their insecurity. This is the same instinct that makes it difficult to apologize when we're wrong so we don't give the other person the imagined "upper hand." This self-protection at the expense of the other person's needs impedes relationship-building, it prevents us from initiating relationships that could be great for us, and it prevents relationships from prospering to a higher trust level because getting our needs met sometimes requires taking risks, which the ego does not like.

Sometimes the ego's competitive drive to keep us alive and valued can push us to be impulsive and emotional. Have you ever thought, "I can't believe I said that!" or "I *shouldn't* have said that"? That's because your ego took over in that moment. It happens to everyone, but if we're going to have great relationships, then we have to recognize when our ego is working against us, and we have to control any competitive impulses that keep us from trying to meet the needs of the people in our lives, both personally and professionally. We have to stop thinking about winning and keep relationship goals in mind.

The goal of relationships should be to partner rather than compete, to collaborate rather than manipulate, to empathize rather than judge, to brainstorm rather than criticize, or to meet a need rather than to win or be right. Sometimes the goal should just be to respectfully acknowledge each other and say hello in the hall. The protective and competitive tendencies of the ego are not needed in these everyday situations. Our level of ability to keep the ego consistently under control and balance our needs with the needs of those around us depends on our maturity level, and will determine our success or failure in every relationship.

PART

2

How You Should Lead Your Relationships: The Five Levels of Maturity

My younger sister and I used to play tricks on each other all the time when we were kids. I am the eleventh child in our family, she is the twelfth (and youngest), and we are only one year apart in age. Everyone else seemed to be grown up and busy while we amused ourselves all day as kids. I remember planning where and when to jump out and scare her. I remember how she "got me back" later. Every time one of us got tricked, we used to say, "You're so immature!" If you have siblings, then you know that the only correct response is "No, *you* are!"

We knew that being called immature was an insult even if we didn't actually know what being mature was. Without being able to explain it we knew that being mature was something *better* than being immature. Maturity was something to aspire to, to grow into. It was something that adults had, that kids didn't. It allowed them to have adult conversations and concerns, while we were always just trying to outdo each other and get attention as the youngest members of a busy household, because as kids you think the world revolves around you. We weren't mature enough to look for each other's needs at that stage. Our parents filled our basic needs, and we sought extra attention and a self-esteem boost by trying to win whatever game we played together that day.

Classic psychology describes the transition of going from the ego-centeredness of toddlerhood and young childhood to other-centeredness once we reach the age of reason, as a progression through critical stages of human development. This indicates that other-centeredness is further along on a human development scale than self-centeredness and is therefore a more appropriate stage of development for adults.

When we can acknowledge, understand, and consider the needs of others, we begin to move into a more adult perspective on life and relationships. However, other-centeredness and maturity does not automatically come along with aging into adulthood. We all know adults who struggle with self-centeredness and immaturity. This stunted development causes relationship problems for them because they cannot, or don't choose to, form healthy relationships based on mutual respect. Instead of building mutually beneficial relationships with others, they use other people as a barometer for their own self-image. They are stuck in a constant doom loop of "how am I doing," and they determine their success or failure by always trying to win at something. But as you read in Chapter 3 on the ego, a relationship based on games of winning and losing will not survive because relationships work only when both people get their needs met.

To have any type of relationship with someone, we must be willing to meet the needs they have that correspond with our level of everyday interaction with them, and in return they must be willing to meet a need we have in our interactions.

Spending three decades in the corporate world, speaking to more than 100,000 people, and hearing the stories of more than 2,000 client companies have given me an incredible opportunity to study people interacting on different levels. I have worked with people across many industries, countries, and education and economic levels. In my observations, all the thousands of interactions in which the ego plays a part fall into five categories. In each of these categories, controlling the ego in order to meet someone's need requires a certain amount of maturity, so I call these categories of interactions the Five Levels of Maturity. The levels address things like how well we consider other people's basic needs, avoid being argumentative, honor our agreements, respect other people's opinions, manage people's strengths and weaknesses, apologize and admit fault when we are wrong, and manage our own and others' vulnerabilities.

Here are the Five Levels of Maturity, covered in detail in the next five chapters:

Level One: Recognizing and Acknowledging People

Level Two: Exchanging Facts and Honoring Agreements

Level Three: Navigating Differing Opinions

Level Four: Playing to Strengths and Working Around Weaknesses

Level Five: Understanding Intrinsic and Extrinsic Motivators

My clients' stories reveal the struggle with these basic aspects of human nature that challenge all of us every day. The first step in leading our relationships toward growth and improvement is being aware of where we are in the process. As we dissect the Five Levels of Maturity, I have no doubt that, at times, you will recognize both yourself and other people in your life on the spectrum of described behaviors. You will probably also notice that some of your relationships may struggle at Level One while others have progressed well beyond that. We will discuss how to manage relationships at each of these levels.

This framework for approaching relationships is not meant to help you take every relationship you have to Level Five. That won't be possible with some people. But it will help you recognize what is going on in your relationships and help you address problems and move beyond them if you are willing to do the work.

Examples of failure at each level depict an interaction between two people, how one person gave in to their ego and turned the interaction into a game of win-lose, and how the need of the other person was not met because of it. Success or failure at each level is determined by whether we let the competitive spirit of the ego take over and turn everything into a game, or whether we see the human being for the need they have in that interaction, and we meet that need. For example, success at Level One means you can move to the next level of interaction with this person with confidence, and thus lead the relationship forward to the next level. Failure at a particular level reveals that this relationship has probably reached its maximum potential and should be managed where it is.

Think of a time when someone in a personal or business relationship left you in disgust at their behavior, made you angry or resentful, hurt you or betrayed you, made you roll your eyes at their pettiness, or otherwise let you down. If you examine what happened, you will most likely find that it was a failure at one of these levels. You will undoubtedly be able to think of an example of when someone could not control their ego in each of these categories. It is so easy to think of times when other people fail at something, but this model is not only for pointing out other people's failures. Have there been times when you were on the other end of this, and you were the one responsible for making someone feel that way? That time it was you who failed to meet the other person's need. I urge you to focus not only on how this can help lead your relationships with others who might be at different maturity levels, but also how this is an opportunity for you to grow your relationships so that you can be more successful and engaged personally and professionally with the people around you.

Mastering the Five Levels of Maturity is the key to improving engagement in every organization, social group, and one-on-one relationship. Being engaged in something means being fully present, in the moment, and completely immersed in what you are doing, creating a rhythm of productivity, growth, and satisfaction. Anything that doesn't make sense in your environment – like relationship games, manipulation, power plays, or any inauthentic behavior – can pose a threat to your security and absorb your attention, breaking you out of that immersion and disrupting engagement.

The Five Levels of Maturity describe behaviors that enhance engagement as the levels progress. When your needs at each of these levels are met, you can focus on work or goals. A problem at each level breaks engagement, turning your attention to the social situation at hand. If you feel disrespected, ignored, threatened, or suspicious of someone's motives, or if you believe you are being lied to, you are getting the silent treatment, or you are otherwise being manipulated, this relationship problem can quickly become the focus of your thoughts. Any of these things can break you out of engagement, preventing concentration on a task or project, and your emotional safety will become your number one priority. All of these things cause disengagement and "quiet quitting," or doing the bare minimum to remain employed and nothing more.

In response to disappointing engagement surveys, many employers have launched fun traditions like hiring food trucks on Fridays or playing Ping-Pong in the lobby in an effort to improve morale and boost engagement. Unfortunately, this does not fix a culture of gossip or ghosting. Instead of pretending everything is functional when it isn't, use the Five Levels of Maturity to identify and address the relationship problems that are hindering engagement in the first place. Harmony, alignment, and mature, nonmanipulative relationships are what create an engaging environment where we can focus on the nature of our work, synergy, productivity, and collaboration.

The Five Levels of Maturity teach accountability for relationship interactions so that you can develop a culture of engagement based on respect and build a business that can focus on serving customers' needs. They start with the most basic requirement of human interaction and progress in complexity from there. Through learning the Five Levels of Maturity that govern our relationships, you can learn how to better manage the egos of other people so that the games people play do not become part of your business culture and interfere with your business mission.

4

Level One: Recognizing and Acknowledging People

The first and most basic relationship need we all have is to be acknowledged by others and recognized when we are in the presence of someone we know. Success at Level One Maturity is meeting that basic need in our relationships regardless of the situation. This is the minimum level of maturity required from everyone in order to build a culture of respect in any business or social group.

> Success at Level One Maturity is recognizing and acknowledging someone we know by making eye contact, greeting them in an appropriate way, and responding to communication as expected.

If you and I know each other or work together, it is customary that when we first see each other we give a greeting like a nod, wink, handshake, fist bump, hug, smile, wave, or a simple "hello," "good morning," or "how are you?" All around the world in every country, culture, and social group, customs are created to address this basic need to be acknowledged by the people we know and interact with regularly. Acknowledging people by saying hello, shaking hands, and making eye contact is part of basic manners taught to children as we teach them kindness and politeness. It isn't difficult, and it's expected.

While success at Level One Maturity seems easy, failure is more common than you might think. Even this basic level of maturity in human interaction can become difficult for people when the ego gets involved. As simple as it sounds, the majority of my clients experience problems with this level of maturity. Many times during our workshops, the employees of a company will report experiencing Level One Maturity failures, and the leaders of the company are not even aware of the microaggressions that take place in their teams. At this level, failures are often symptoms of bigger, company-wide problems like poor hiring decisions or disengaged leaders. When clients tell me they are having engagement or morale issues, games of power and punishment at Level One Maturity usually come with it. People will have trouble engaging in a culture that allows games of the ego to prevail over respect and teamwork.

Let the Games Begin!

I won't ask, "Have you ever been in this situation?" because I know everyone has. You greet a classmate, neighbor, colleague, or even a close friend, and instead of the usual greeting, they ignore you, refuse eye contact, or give you a cold half-smile in return. That is not what you expected. What's wrong? Some people might dismiss this as that person having a bad day or perhaps being deep in thought and not realizing that they were being rude. Some people might quickly reflect on the relationship and recent interactions to see if you can point to anything wrong between you. Either way, most people would notice this as something that is disordered. Either they didn't see or hear you, and so they accidentally ignored your greeting, or they did it on purpose. If the person purposely ignored your greeting, either consciously or subconsciously, then they failed to show Level One Maturity in your relationship that day.

Withholding that recognition and acknowledgment from someone for any reason is sending a message that ego has taken over and this person is playing a game by ignoring you and attempting to make you feel confused or insignificant to them, which means they win, and you lose. I know this seems petty and childish as you read it, but we could fill this book with examples of these failures and the kind of games people play with Level One Maturity in the regular course of business.

Failure at Level One is often portrayed in movies or TV as socially deviant, bullying, or mean-spirited adolescent behavior. How many movies about high school drama involve the popular kid who will only acknowledge the protagonist when others aren't around, and then when the popular crowd arrives, the antagonist pretends not to know the protagonist exists? Then there is the opposite, more passive-aggressive style of bullying, where someone will be nice to the protagonist in front of other people, only to ignore them or worse when no one else is around. Most people recognize this as a familiar stereotype and have had the unfortunate experience of someone pretending not to know who they are or denying eye contact or a hello as they pass on the street, on campus, or in the hallway.

This is a power play using acknowledgment and recognition as a weapon. It is meant to convey the idea that you know who they are because they are *important*, but they do not know who you are because you are *unimportant*. It's *I don't acknowledge you; you acknowledge me*. It's meant to send a message: you are not on my level. And you wouldn't want to be on their level because they are failing at Level One Maturity.

While this stereotypical mean-spirited behavior might be common in adolescent stories, it's not limited to middle school and high school or even college, and it's not just fictional. Adults are just as susceptible to this kind of inclination in any social or business groups. In fact, someone's level of maturity is not necessarily commensurate with age, experience, or even education.

One of my clients is a major health system in a metropolitan area and is having a problem with Level One Maturity among its employees. In their case, it's not the hourly wage earners who are causing the problem. Believe it or not, the biggest offenders are a certain group of doctors, which includes both men and women. Some of the most educated people at this health system will not make eye contact with subordinates in the hall, will not acknowledge people who walk into a room, and have created an air of elitism and professional hierarchy that is making it difficult for people who work in their departments to do their jobs. Even some of the surgical nurses have expressed that they feel intimidated in the operating room. This health system has had to take time out from their business of saving lives for its professional employees to receive coaching and training on the Five Levels of Maturity and how success or failure at each level can affect people's ability to do their jobs well and can ultimately impact the effectiveness and culture of a business as well as its bottom line.

Another of my clients is a tech company whose VP of sales will only interact with the sales reps who are hitting their numbers. His public approval of them is demonstrated through greetings and joking around and public conversations in the office about their kids or their weekend plans. In private he admits that he uses this as a motivator for those who are underperforming to step up their sales. However, the reps who are left out can see that he only talks to the reps who are making money for him, and he refuses to help or spend time with newer or struggling reps so they can learn the job, thereby making it impossible for them to break into the next level of success at the company. The company is carrying the salaries of these reps without seeing much of a return. They incur high turnover costs in that department. The accounts assigned to these reps are underserved and not impressed with the company, and as a result the customer retention rate is affected. The atmosphere of ego, competition, games, and disrespect takes a toll on the noncommission employees in the department as well.

One client hired me to provide a Leading Relationships workshop for her team after she had been promoted from within the department. She said once she was promoted, she was no longer welcome at her former lunch table, and she got the silent treatment when approaching her former teammates talking in the hall. The overall atmosphere of resentment and unspoken hostility was not only threatening the team's ability to work together, but the employees probably did not realize it was also threatening their jobs because she did not intend to continue allowing that atmosphere to persist. These employees let their egos take over and they were playing a win-lose game with their new boss. In their eyes, they were jealous that she won the promotion, so they would make her lose her friendships in the office and her peace at work by creating hostility. Just as employees have a need to be acknowledged and not ignored by their managers, she had the same need to be acknowledged and not ignored by her subordinate team. If they continued to disrespect her by playing these win-lose games, they would most likely lose their jobs.

In my experience, people are aware that this type of behavior is not honorable. This was proven to me once when John, a long-time client, referred me to his friend for sales training. I contacted the friend, saying "John referred me to you" several times in voice mails and emails over the course of about three months, with no response. When John asked me if I ever worked with him, I simply said, "No, it didn't work out. He never got back to me." You can probably guess what happened next. I got an angry voicemail from the friend saying he didn't appreciate that I "badmouthed" him to John. In other words, when his own behavior was presented in plain facts, he was embarrassed by it and angry that he was called out on it.

I have clients who report stories of Hollywood directors mistreating set employees, executives mistreating assistants, sports figures mistreating their team employees, and even family-owned businesses mistreating each other or nonfamily employees. Some people with positions of power see denying acknowledgment and recognition to those below them on the ladder as a "privilege" of power, like a hazing rite of passage. Some of these people have practiced for this for their whole career. There are body language experts who teach people how to purposely establish a position of power in ways like who says hello first, who extends their hand first, how firm is the handshake, whose hand is on top, who breaks eye contact first, how long is the handshake, who lets go first, and how to restrict access to you via direct phone or email.

These positional power games take root right from the beginning of the relationship. They reveal what these things say about perceived worth and power. It's exhausting for normal people to think about, and it's misleading to the people listening to it who are deceived into thinking that in the long run power is more valuable to their careers than building good relationships and having a reputation of maturity and human kindness. They are trying to build their own self-image on being better than someone else, instead of on their own accomplishments and abilities and value as a human being.

When someone plays these games, it interferes with their ability to be sincere and to genuinely connect with others. They are choosing competition and dominance over relationships and connections. All of those techniques usually communicate to the other person that this is someone they should try to avoid, and that's usually the point. If someone is trying to convey power or intimidation, then they want you to stay away from their territory, so oblige them because you can't expect even Level One Maturity from them.

What If Everything Isn't Fine Between Us?

To most of us this type of power play by adolescent bullies or corporate climbers is a familiar story about other people behaving badly, but sometimes failure at Level One is a lot closer to home than that. It's easy to be mature and polite, say hello, and meet people's basic needs when everything is fine between us, but when we have a problem, the ego can complicate even the most basic interactions between two people who have a good relationship, and drive us to deny acknowledgment and recognition as punishment for the problem.

For example, on a normal day your colleague would arrive at work and see you in the hall and say hello. Let's say later that day in a meeting you disagree with that same colleague about how a new procedure should work, and your solution is chosen over theirs. The next morning you see your colleague in the hall, and they don't say hello, or don't say hello back if you greeted them first, or they tone down their usual friendly greeting slightly, so you wonder if something is wrong.

Have you ever been angry with someone who texted you, so you ghosted them without telling them why? Have you ever had a problem with a colleague at work so that you took longer than you should have to respond to their email, or you didn't give them all the information they needed so that they had to do more work? Have you ever decided not to get up and greet a new colleague because you were resentful that they got hired instead of the company promoting you? Have you ever given someone close to you the silent treatment because you were upset, and you wanted them to know it? Have you ever pulled back from a friend or cut them off without explanation because you were feeling jealous or resentful, or you were feeling dissatisfied with your own life at a time when they were prospering? Have you ever been the recipient of this type of behavior?

In all these scenarios, someone withheld acknowledgment and recognition as punishment for a negative feeling they experienced in these situations, even if it wasn't necessarily the other person's fault. It's important to realize that these actions said the following about that person:

- "I measure my self-worth by how I size up against other people."

- "My self-worth took a hit because you disagreed with me or won something over me (including the approval of others)."

- "I can regain some of that self-worth by being too good to say hello to you, and making you feel foolish or unimportant or guilty for hurting me directly or indirectly."

Whether it's a colleague in the hall or a friend or family member, when we approach things like exchanging basic courtesy and respect with a competitive spirit, we are letting the ego take over and applying that competitive spirit at an inappropriate time in order to either seek revenge for a perceived hurt, seek protection from a perceived threat, or establish dominance over a perceived competitor. We are turning our basic interactions with other human beings into a game of win-lose, and then denying their basic need for acknowledgment to either get even or to go for the win. Whether that is done as a power play or a punishment, it is a failure at Level One Maturity and that competitive spirit is weakening or even destroying our existing relationships and our potential for new relationships, which weakens our ability to be effective in our careers.

You Don't Automatically Start at Level One, You Have to Reach It

Level One is actually not a starting place for everyone. It's something you have to reach by consistently showing respect for the human dignity of others by recognizing and acknowledging people you know in appropriate day-to-day situations, and not letting your ego take over and play games by withholding this respect from others.

In business and personal relationships, you cannot move on with the relationship until you can trust someone to be consistent at Level One. You can't share opinions, you can't make agreements, you can't show vulnerability, you can't work together or live together successfully until you can trust someone to act with Level One Maturity all the time. If you don't know when you will get the silent treatment, when someone will embarrass you by ignoring you in front of other people, when someone will try to make you feel small by pretending that they don't know who you are, then you can't have a successful relationship with them, and your interactions with them have to be managed and limited.

The bottom line is you should always maintain Level One Maturity in any situation. Even if someone else fails at Level One, you take the high road.

There is only one mature way to handle someone who is not acknowledging you, or not meeting you at Level One. The lesson to remember is that your job is never to go below Level One Maturity yourself in any situation, even if someone else does. If the other person doesn't meet you there, you can stay at Level One, not less, not more. This way you are not showing disrespect to anyone, you are exhibiting basic courtesy and maturity, which maintains your professional reputation, and you are also not engaging in acknowledgment games. As with most things, this is easier said than done.

My friend Mary had to use this lesson in her own neighborhood. Her next-door neighbor, Christine, began the silent treatment out of the blue one day. Mary would say hi when she saw Christine outside, and Christine would pretend she didn't hear Mary. It went on for a while without explanation. They used to be friendly, so Mary wondered why Christine was being rude, and she eventually started avoiding being outside at the same time as Christine because it was awkward. But when the nice elderly lady across the street was outside, Christine would initiate and say hi to Mary in front of the other lady. Christine acted friendly in front of the neighbor lady, which she knew would confuse Mary, so Christine wins, but if Mary ignored her greeting out of spite, then Christine looks good in front of the nice lady *and* Mary looks bad, and Christine wins two ways.

Christine is playing a game using acknowledgment and recognition. Mary doesn't want to play. Her job is to say hi back to Christine regardless of her behavior, especially because the neighbor lady doesn't know what's going on between them. If Mary shows her frustration at Christine for being fake by snubbing her in return, then the neighbor lady's only takeaway is that Mary is the nasty person for not being nice to Christine. If Mary wants to protect her good reputation with the neighbor lady, then she must reciprocate the greeting and take the high road.

Mary does not have the responsibility to punish Christine's behavior. That would only backfire on her. Mary can't control Christine's behavior; she can only honor her own value of never going below Level One Maturity, even if Christine does. If Christine acts like this in a neighbor relationship, then she probably acts like this in other relationships as well, and she has probably faced consequences for it somewhere. Mary does not want to be a part of that. She should limit her communication with this person, and the easiest way to do that is to maintain Level One Maturity. If Mary tries to give Christine the silent treatment in return or "stoop to her level," then she has engaged in Christine's game, and that is the opposite of Mary's goal of having pleasant interactions with people. If Mary just continues to say hi to Christine when Christine initiates in front of the other neighbors and gives Christine the space she wants when no one else is around, then Mary maintains a safe distance from Christine. Mary knows how Christine handles relationships now; she does not want to be connected to Christine. If Mary maintains Level One Maturity even when Christine does not, it shows that Mary understands Christine is playing a game and Mary declines the invitation to play along. No thank you, Christine, Mary is fine over here at Level One.

If someone has made it known that they don't want you to acknowledge them, even in a non-passive-aggressive way, then you can maintain Level One by respecting their space and only greeting them when it would be inappropriate *not to*, as in if they talk to you first, or if you make eye contact, and then you can just give them a smile. You don't want to force communication with them. Only greet them when it would be inappropriate for you *not* to greet them.

Are You Saying . . .

There are a few questions that frequently come up in my workshops. My answer is the same for each one: use your head and don't play games; your intentions matter. Here are the most frequently asked questions I get regarding Level One:

Are you saying I should go around all day saying hi to everyone I see multiple times per day? No. Just use your head and don't play games. Greet people according to the customs in your office or social group. Your intentions matter. If you specifically do not want to say hi to someone, what is your reason? If it's because you don't want to bother them while they're busy or for some other legitimate reason, that's fine. If it's because you want to convey that you are more important than they are, or you don't want them to know that you recognize them, that's your ego being threatened and taking over, and you need to control that.

Are you saying I am only mature if I say hi to every stranger walking down the street? No. Level One Maturity is acknowledgment and recognition of people *you know*. Aside from common courtesy such as saying thank you when someone holds a door for you, you don't have to greet every stranger you pass on the street; in fact, that doesn't sound safe. In a city or close quarters like an elevator or a train, there are unwritten rules regarding respecting people's personal space, where it is more polite not to speak at all. In a more open community, strangers will frequently greet each other walking down the street as a courtesy. Countries other than the United States may have different rules and customs around greetings. Again, your intentions matter. Are you not saying hi to someone because it is not culturally necessary or appropriate in that situation? Or is it because you believe you are too important to say hello to them? Don't play ego games with acknowledgment and recognition.

Are you saying I have to talk to everyone, even someone who has hurt me to the point where I do not want them to be a part of my life anymore? No. If someone poses a threat to your physical safety or mental health, I don't think you need me to tell you to create a boundary for yourself and not to interact with this person anymore. Level One Maturity addresses how we relate to people we know without letting our ego take over and how we use acknowledgment and recognition as weapons of power-positioning or punishment in order to make us feel better about our own lives and choices.

Are you saying I have to greet my chatty colleague every morning and get stuck in a long conversation with her? Not exactly – you don't have to seek out someone who doesn't respect other people's time and greet them, thus giving them dominion over your time. We all know people like this. They don't understand Level One Maturity, and they take your greeting as an opportunity to engage in conversation when it isn't welcome or appropriate to do so. You don't have time for that. It's OK to walk down an alternate hallway to avoid running into someone like this. However, you do have to return their greeting if they greet you first. If you make eye contact with this person and you're in a situation where it would be impolite or disrespectful to walk away, stay at Level One Maturity and say hello.

The art of excusing yourself from a conversation you don't have time for is called "managing interruptions," and that is a skill I teach in my Personal Leadership workshop, also covered in my book *Decide*. The key to it is that when you have an opportunity to speak, you should respond to something the other person said, and then interrupt *yourself*, rather than the other person, which would be rude. It might sound something like this: "Oh wow, it sounds like you had such a nice weekend, I would like to try that restaurant sometime. . . . Oh, I have to get started on this assignment though, so have a great day!" Or in a social situation: ". . . I promised my friend I would come right back after I got my plate. Enjoy the party!" Or something similar. It takes a little practice, and you may or may not pull it off every time, but learning how to politely excuse yourself from a conversation you don't have time for is an essential personal and professional skill. The key is interrupting *yourself* in mid-sentence, not the other person, and that way you maintain respectful communication with them.

What has been your experience when joining a new organization or a new team? Were you greeted with kindness and openness, or given the cold shoulder? Did your new colleagues go out of their way to meet your need to be acknowledged and welcomed, or were you sent a clear message that your presence was a threat to their status in the hierarchy? Think of the last time someone joined your team, social group, or neighborhood. How did you do? Did you go out of your way to welcome them and meet their need for acceptance, or did you start playing games by intentionally not acknowledging them to send a message?

Take a minute to think about the different groups or relationships in your personal and professional life. Does each of them operate at Level One Maturity consistently? Do you know if you will get a sincere greeting or if someone will try to make you feel invisible in order to build themselves up at any given time? Without this basic level of respect and courtesy, it can be difficult for the relationship to continue. If this is happening in a particular group or setting you are involved in, it's your job not to give in to the immature games being played. You must continue to exhibit Level One Maturity and meet people's basic need for acknowledgment and recognition, regardless of the occasional games being played by the other person, or any problems that may exist between you.

If someone is withholding recognition and acknowledgment to play games of power or punishment, it can be damaging to your business or group culture. In Chapter 5 you will learn the Broken Agreement Script, which can be used to address this.

Level One Quick Reference Guide

Success at Level One Maturity is recognizing and acknowledging someone we know by making eye contact, greeting them in an appropriate way, and responding to communication as expected. If someone displays Level One Maturity successfully, you can progress to Level Two interactions confidently.

Failure at Level One Maturity is playing games of *punishment* like ghosting on electronic communication, giving the silent treatment, or conducting *power plays* like waiting for the other person to say hello first, pretending not to recognize someone or remember their name, or ignoring them.

How to proceed with the relationship if someone fails at Level One Maturity: Since this is a foundational level of maturity, you must maintain at least Level One Maturity with everyone in your life and everyone you meet, including anyone you are required to work with, even if they fail at this level. If they fail to treat you with a basic level of maturity and respect, then you should limit your interactions with them as much as possible. This is not someone you can trust or with whom you can build a stronger relationship. Regardless of their failure to exhibit basic maturity, your job is never to fail at Level One Maturity with anyone. Your personal reputation should always be to maintain this basic level of respectful behavior.

Skill learned: Always maintain this basic level of maturity by treating everyone with respect and dignity and not withholding recognition and acknowledgment.

Level Two: Exchanging Facts and Honoring Agreements

There are two things we are responsible for at Level Two Maturity: exchanging facts and honoring our agreements. They are at the same level of mature interaction because of a common thread. A deliberate failure at, or refusal to cooperate with, either of these two interactions usually stems from a decision to be a "difficult" person.

Success at Level Two Maturity is exchanging facts and information efficiently, keeping facts in context without misrepresenting or twisting them, answering questions earnestly, and honoring the agreements that we make either explicitly or implicitly.

Business interactions require a minimum of Level Two Maturity. To do business together, we need to be able to exchange facts and make agreements confidently on varying levels of importance to our business. Whether it's a simple agreement like submitting an expense report on time, or a large client contract, we cannot do business together unless we can share information and honor our agreements.

Level Two is trust in action. It's doing what you said you would do without being a difficult person.

Exchanging Facts

A fact is a fact; it's irrefutable, undeniable, evidence-based information. Yesterday's weather, stock market performance, and the score of last night's game are facts. We can't change them or argue them.

Even if I don't like you, I can't argue when you say it was 75 degrees yesterday in our city. If you state an evidence-based fact, I would have to agree with you, right? What if I would rather do anything in the world except agree with you on anything? Would you agree that if I really wanted to, I could find a way to disagree with anything you say even if it is a "fact"?

Facts are usually expressed within a context. If I want to argue with something, all I have to do is change the context and then I can argue with the "fact." When you said yesterday was the warmest day ever recorded for that date in history, the context was that you meant in a particular location, at the warmest part of the day, as recorded by modern meteorological means that track weather patterns back to the late 1800s (yes, that was a quick internet search and you could argue with me if you want to). When you said that the team won by three points last night, you meant the actual score of the game. I changed the context to include the predictions of sports writers and gamblers. When you said our stock is up 10% over this time last year, you were doing simple math using the closing stock prices on two dates. I suggested you use additional data. If I change the context, then your fact becomes arguable, even if it's just to clarify the context you were using. I am just trying to make you work harder, to frustrate you, or to make myself look smarter than you.

A client in the insurance industry just took on a leadership role on a new team. The team has an assistant who was hired by the department director and has been at the company for her whole career. Whether out of resentment, self-esteem issues, or something else entirely, the assistant must always be right, and everyone treads carefully around her. If someone says, "It's warm out today," she'll say, "not in Alaska." If someone says their team won last night she'll say, "But they didn't beat the spread, so you would have lost that bet." Her commitment to being difficult knows no boundaries. Team members have given up on small talk when she's in the room and have invented their own work-around procedures to get things done without her involvement, and avoiding those extra tasks could be her goal. This creates an uncomfortable work environment and limits any team bonding that the new leader can facilitate. Not only does she twist facts just to be difficult, but the company also has a value of respect and clear communication, which she is clearly not honoring.

One company decided to have a leadership retreat for their executives at a beautiful resort, and they hired me to do a keynote speech for them. One of the executives had voted against spending the money on the retreat and even though he was outvoted, he attended anyway. He complained about every meal, service, and amenity at the pristine resort during the whole weekend. He wanted to make sure that no one enjoyed their stay too much and that he was relevant to the weekend even though he had been outvoted.

Another client invited me to give a presentation in a conference room in their office on the top floor of a high-rise building. The beautiful city view through the floor-to-ceiling windows and the high leatherback chairs at the long conference table made for an impressive setting. The person who opened the meeting had a 15-minute slot before my presentation to give a few in-house updates. A few minutes into his presentation he shared a simple fact about the business, which another board member disputed. Sides were taken and for the next 10 minutes these high-powered exec-utives argued like children until all the time for his presentation was used, and he didn't get a chance to finish.

This is failing at Level Two Maturity. Whether that person is angry over something or they are just being difficult for any reason, they decided that whatever you say they will find a way to make you wrong, or to demonstrate that they know more about the topic at hand than you do. They're trying to win at exchanging facts. This is the ego taking over and inserting competition in a basic interaction. If you work together or live together or have an essential relationship of any kind, this is going to be difficult to manage. I can feel the eye rolls coming. You will have to clarify the context of all facts and information, which takes more work and time, but this is what is necessary to do business with them.

What are the reasons that people act this way? It could be very similar to why people fail at Level One Maturity. They may be trying to punish you for something that made them upset. Maybe they feel disrespected, taken for granted, inferior, under-valued, or jealous. They may be making a power play between the two of you, trying to make you wrong or to appear more knowledgeable about something in order to make you feel inferior to them in some way. Even if they aren't doing it on purpose to gain power, perhaps they get self-esteem from always being right, knowing more than others, or demonstrating intelligence or knowledge in front of others. Some people are even afraid that they will seem uneducated if they receive information from others, so they argue and push back at everything that comes their way. Whatever switch was flipped in their personality, they decided to become difficult. They now make every interaction between you difficult, which accomplishes their goal. If they were to say it out loud, it would sound something like this:

> *"My ego is hurt, so in retaliation, I will make sure that everyone wastes time and stops progress."*

To be successful at this level would be civilly exchanging facts and information with each other. That's it! If you can do this without arbitrarily challenging each other, without the need to make the other person wrong or to know more than the other person in order to make them feel inferior, regardless of how you feel about the other person and without your ego getting in the way, then you have succeeded at the first part of Level Two Maturity.

Most people in most situations will succeed at this part of Level Two and not have the urge to argue with someone over a fact as long as that fact is correct by all standards, but if the information presented is actually incorrect it gets more difficult.

If you are telling a story and you get a detail wrong, is it necessary for me to interrupt and correct you? What if there were several people present? The answer should depend on whether the detail is consequential to the story and also on the setting of the situation. If the point of your story is about a funny thing you saw happen and you say it happened on Monday, but I know it was Tuesday, that detail doesn't matter to the story. You're trying to make me laugh and build our relationship by engaging in fun conversation with me and interrupting you to correct an inconsequential detail tells you that I am not that interested in your story; I am more interested in being right than in listening to you and building our relationship. The mature thing to do would be to let it go because your need is for me to value you and respect your effort to engage with me more than I value the accuracy of an irrelevant detail. However, some people can't let anything go regardless of whether or not it matters. If their ego is threatened for some reason, they may choose to value being right over possibly hurting your feelings. They see this as a chance to correct you and let you know that having the right information, even if it is trivial, is more important to them than you are. If you have a fragile or new relationship, this could damage it or could damage your opinion of them as a potential friend. Even if you have an established relationship, acting like this could send a message that you can't count on them to recognize and take care of your needs in any situation since they allowed their ego to take over and they valued being right over allowing you to tell a funny story and laugh together.

What if we're not talking about a funny story but rather an important conversation about business, and what if the information that you got wrong is not trivial, but rather is important to our conversation? There are situations when correcting someone is necessary. Intentions come through here. Be mindful of the relationship and make sure the person knows they are more important than the data, but the data has to be corrected. By respecting the person as much as the accuracy of the information, and by not taking the opportunity to make me look bad, you have just built trust not only with me but also with everyone who heard you do that.

Honoring Agreements

This is where commerce happens. Commerce is a series of agreements. It happens when we both do what we said we would do. I'll give you 10 dollars, and you give me a sandwich. That's business. If I don't give you the 10 dollars when you've made the sandwich, or if you don't give me the sandwich after I've given you the 10 dollars, then we can't do business together anymore.

> Commerce can happen only when people keep their agreements.

That's a simple way of looking at it. You may not realize that each detail of your job is an agreement that you have made with your employer. A job description describes what an employer wants an employee to do, and the values of your organization describe how, or with what intentions, the employer wants those things to be done. The employee agrees to all of that in exchange for the salary they get paid. The problem is they don't take that salary and distribute it to all the little things they do for their job in order to put an individual value on each of those tasks.

They don't get emails that come with a payment of 50 cents for their response; if they did, they would see each of those tasks for how valuable they are to the organization. They are getting paid to respond to those emails as part of their salary. If they don't respond, they are taking the money for doing the job, and then not doing the job. They are taking the 10 dollars and not making the sandwich. This diminishes the organization's trust in them, and it will be reflected in the success of their business.

The same is true if they aren't living up to the values of the organization. Before entering the business world, we've never been paid to treat someone a certain way. It is possible to thrive academically in school or on an athletic field and also be rude and condescending, but if I take a job with an organization that has company values of treating others with respect and honoring the agreements I make, then I am actually getting paid to treat people the way I want to be treated. I am not just agreeing to complete my job duties, but also to do the job in a way consistent with the company values. If you got a check in the mail every two weeks based on how well you treated your family members or your neighbors, how much better would you treat them? By taking this job I have made an agreement to abide by my organization's values. It is an implicit agreement that I can be held accountable for, and that includes how I treat people at work.

In Chapter 2 we discussed that always doing what you say you are going to do is what maintains trust in a relationship. This is not only necessary for any one-on-one relationship to thrive, but also for successful commerce as well. Your business partners, customers, employees, vendors, superiors, and subordinates all need to have confidence that when you make an agreement you will follow through, and if you fail to follow through for some reason you will acknowledge it and apologize. This is what trust means in business.

We make lots of agreements on a daily basis. We agree to respond to each other's emails, to show up on time for meetings, and many other day-to-day interactions. It's easy to follow through on an agreement with my boss or a customer because there are implied consequences to not following through, but what about someone who can't hold me accountable, like a subordinate, or a vendor, or even a friend? Many times, someone in a position of power in the relationship doesn't follow through on an agreement simply because they know they cannot be held accountable for it. For example, a subordinate who needs a paycheck may accept the disrespect of a broken agreement from their boss, or a salesperson who needs to close a sale may repeatedly accept broken commitments of missed phone appointments or extended wait times from a customer. The boss and the customer have positional power in those relationships, and they are using it to take advantage of the people who are trying to do business with them. This is failure at Level Two Maturity. They are playing games and letting their ego take over when they should have fair and ethical business practices. This is not a sustainable way of doing business, and the lack of confidence that this inspires will likely have consequences, including high employee turnover, decreased customer retention, increased legal costs, and increased human resources costs. It's not just business; this can happen in any relationship where there is a perceived "upper hand."

A lot of conflict happens at Level Two when people don't do what they say they are going to do, and they don't acknowledge it and apologize for it. Your confidence in them is decreased, and your relationship can be threatened. If someone frequently does not follow through on their agreements by doing what they said they would do, you will need to either address the issue with them or cease relying on them for anything important, including doing business together.

Addressing Broken Agreements Without Damaging the Relationship

The ability to hold people accountable for their agreements without damaging the relationship is one of the most valuable skills a business leader can have. This skill will help you resolve conflicts between employer and employee, and also between colleagues, encouraging stronger relationships with less drama to develop.

With so many relationships and agreements in our daily lives, the likelihood of someone breaking an agreement with you at some point is fairly high. These situations can be complex and difficult because we should desire compliance with agreements but also harmony in relationships. Those two things can seem to be mutually exclusive when someone breaks an agreement because calling out their noncompliance with what they said they would do can be detrimental to the relationship if not handled correctly. However, if I have broken an agreement with you and every time I see you I feel discomfort over it, then that will negatively affect our relationship as well. Knowing how to handle it in the moment can prevent stress, clear up confusion, and possibly save the relationship if it is handled correctly.

So many times when I visit a client and talk to them about culture issues in the office, they tell me stories of one employee or another who is causing an issue, a group of employees who are resisting a change in procedure, employees showing up to work late, gossip in employee circles about other employees or about management, the "real" meeting being in the hall after the meeting, or some other example of unproductive or problematic behavior. I have heard the word "babysitting" mentioned almost as many times in office discussions with my clients as I have in my own house while raising four children. Most stories of people not getting along can be dissected into "he said, she said" and go around and around forever without resolution.

Although these situations can be complex, at their root they usually involve a plain and simple broken agreement. When an employee is hired by a company, that employee agrees to abide by their job description, along with the company's mission, vision, values, and goals, whether that agreement is explicitly stated or implicitly implied. They agree to do a certain job in a certain way that is in line with the company mission. That's a simple agreement, and the consequences of not abiding by the agreement should be clearly stated and understood by all parties.

When people do not honor their agreements in business, a leader must hold them accountable and course-correct that behavior, or else more examples of the same behavior will follow from that person and others who observe the situation. This is true of small infractions like being late for work, as well as more impactful problems like honoring contract terms. Knowing how to address the broken agreement with the goal of correcting the behavior is a crucial leadership and life skill that helps to simplify and resolve these complex situations.

Establishing an agreement can be as simple as stating the desired behavior or action and asking for verbal agreement. For example, when a new procedure is introduced for a team to follow, buy-in should be verbally requested by the team leader, and then they have a plain and simple agreement. Subsequently, if the new procedures are not followed, there is an agreement in place that can be referenced so it can be upheld. Another example is that every meeting leader should create ground rules, including a request that team members give feedback within the meeting, so everyone knows what is going on. Then they have a plain and simple agreement. If there is gossip after the meeting, then the broken agreement can be addressed easily.

We make little agreements every day. When you drive a car, you agree to every rule of the road in whatever state or country you are in. When you join a Wi-Fi network, you check "I agree" to the terms and conditions of that network before they let you join. When you make an online account on any retailer's website, you agree to their policies, terms, and conditions. When you go to the beach or the dog park, there are posted rules of use. When you join any organized group, there are rules of behavior that you agree to by becoming a member. When you are seated in an exit row on an airplane, they ask for your verbal agreement to assist in an emergency. When I facilitate my workshops, I always start with a list of ground rules for the day and ask for a thumbs up from everyone to establish agreement from the group.

Everyone is accustomed to these types of "rules of use" agreements in daily life, so it should be expected that every work team should have them too. With this in mind, the most effective thing that a project team can do is to make a list of ground rules of how they will work together. This creates an agreement that can then be referenced if problems arise. Ideally this agreement for acceptable team behavior should be in place from the beginning of the project or team creation, but if there isn't one in place for an existing team, then it's better to add one mid-project than to proceed without one. I have seen work groups who will be working long hours on an upcoming project together actually create a list of pet peeves from past projects so they can avoid those annoyances and arguments in the future when deadlines heighten the tension in the room. The point of having these agreements in place is to help avoid problems in the first place.

Here is a list of team rules that I helped one of my clients compose:

Project Ground Rules and Team Rules We Live By

- Meetings will start and end on time and have an agenda.
- Respond to meeting requests ASAP or within 24 hours.
- We follow through on what we say we are going to do. If we fail in this, we take responsibility, apologize, and make it right.
- The real meeting takes place during the meeting and not out in the hallway after the meeting.
- We use "yes and" not "yes but" so we can build upon each other's ideas, not tear them down.
- There are no dumb questions.
- If you have a problem or an issue with someone, bring it to them first. If you are unable to resolve it, then ask for help.
- We speak about our colleagues when they are not around the same way we speak about them when they are around.
- We treat each other the way we would like to be treated. If we fail in this, we apologize. If anyone witnessed us treating someone else disrespectfully, we owe them an apology as well.
- We never speak disrespectfully of the customer we serve.
- Never throw a team member under the bus. If you have 1% responsibility in what happened, take it and own it.

- A team is only as strong as its weakest relationship. We concentrate on each other's strengths and work around weaknesses. If we can't work around them, we give feedback to improve them.

- We will never say "It's not my job!" and we'll never be happy to say "no."

Once acceptable behaviors and responsibilities are recognized as agreements, then we can recognize that an unacceptable behavior does, in fact, break those agreements.

When someone breaks an agreement with you, whether it's personal or professional, and they don't try to fix it, the relationship foundation may be cracked, and the amount of resulting damage will depend on the severity of the broken agreement. If you can't let it go and it continues to bother you, but you shy away from actually discussing it, those thoughts will create distance and mistrust. The other person can feel that too. This is how relationships grow apart because it makes trust difficult, if not impossible.

A broken agreement doesn't have to end a relationship, but it should be addressed in order for the relationship to continue in a healthy and functional way. Ignoring a broken agreement or pretending it didn't happen won't work in the long run. Unresolved problems can get in the way of the relationship continuing and usually become the reason people no longer talk to each other or struggle with communication from that point forward, because they are always thinking of something they are not saying. If something is important enough to continue bothering you every time you see this person, or if their professional performance will continue to be affected by it, then it should be addressed in order for your relationship to continue normally, and it should be done respectfully.

Once the broken agreement has been identified, your goal should be to address it and hold that person accountable in such a way that the behavior will change and then business can continue afterwards, and you don't damage your relationship with that person. Sounds tricky, right?

> No one likes to have their poor behavior pointed out and corrected by someone else.

If your goal is not to fix the situation and reestablish the agreement so you can move on respectfully, but rather to admonish and embarrass the other person out of anger, resentment, jealousy, competition, or exasperation, then no script that I give you will validate your motives or fix that relationship. At that point you are essentially preparing to end the relationship rather than fix it. The only way to fix it is to approach the person with the goal of continuing a mutually respectful and healthy relationship afterwards. This can be done by following a simple script with simple ground rules, which I am about to give to you. If you understand the psychology behind the script, then you can tweak it according to your own style, language, or group culture. You also might have to tweak the script according to who you are talking to because you might approach your employee, your boss, a colleague, a vendor, a neighbor, or a friend in slightly different ways. The script taps into what someone with a healthy, age-appropriate level of maturity and reason might be feeling when they break an agreement. It's called cognitive dissonance.

> When your actions, decisions, or behaviors are out of alignment with your agreements or beliefs, it creates the stress, discomfort, and anxiety that psychology calls *cognitive dissonance*.

A psychologically healthy person is likely to feel this stress and anxiety when they believe or say one thing and do another. An easy example of this is when I am driving at 60 mph in a 45 mph zone. If I know I am breaking the law, then I will likely experience cognitive dissonance. There are three ways people normally respond to this situation and attempt to rid themselves of the cognitive dissonance which they created themselves.

Using my case as an example, I will either:

- **Align** my behavior with my agreement or belief. This involves acknowledging and correcting the misaligned behavior. When I reduce my speed to 45mph, I am no longer in cognitive dissonance, and the stress will disappear.

- **Rationalize** why it is okay to drive 60 mph in a 45 mph zone. This is either an internal narrative or a defensive explanation to someone else. For example, *I'm just keeping up with traffic, everyone else is driving this fast, there are no police on this road, cars are safer today than when that speed limit was imposed, no one else is on the road at this hour, I know this road better than anyone else, that speed limit is artificially low for this road for no reason,* *where I have to be is more important than following that rule.* I am rationalizing why it is okay that my actions are out of alignment with the agreement I made when I got a driver's license, which is to follow the laws of the road. Rationalization suppresses cognitive dissonance; it doesn't get rid of it.

- **Deny** knowledge that I ever made an agreement. Again, this could be an internal narrative or a defensive explanation to someone else. For example, if stopped by the police I might say, *What is the speed limit on this road? I didn't see a sign, I didn't know the speed limit; if I did I would have followed it.*

We see examples of this all the time in business when someone has broken an agreement. Employees who are late for work might either apologize and then align their behavior by being on time the next day, they might rationalize by giving excuses as to why they were late, or they might deny that the agreement was broken by saying *It was only a few minutes,* or *We aren't even open for customers yet,* or *I thought we had a flexible start time.*

When an agreement is broken, acknowledgment and alignment make up the mature and honest response. If someone jeopardized a relationship or a job by breaking an agreement, they have to decide if they are more interested in saving it or in upholding their ego. If they want to preserve the relationship (or the job), they will apologize and commit to aligning their behavior in the future. The purpose of an apology is to restore trust and confidence that they can interact reasonably and maturely. This response rebuilds trust because they are acknowledging the broken agreement and not playing games with you. Of course, if ego gets in the way, then they won't bring this conversation to you; they will ignore it and unfortunately leave it up to you to address it, and you might get rationalization or denial as a response if you address the broken agreement with them. The future of the relationship could depend on the outcome of this conversation.

The Broken Agreement Script: The Four-Part Response for Addressing a Broken Agreement

You can use the following script to address a broken agreement and make it easier for the person to respond with alignment, and possibly also an apology, if appropriate for the situation. This script makes the conversation as direct and brief as possible and therefore less painful for both of you.

Part 1

Create safety and security by asking for their help. This is an effective way to start the conversation. It indicates that you are trying to work with them to solve a problem, not simply convict them of wrongdoing. You are asking for their involvement in finding a solution. When someone asks for your help with something, it is normally disarming; it suggests that you will be working on the same side of an issue rather than putting the other person on the defensive, and it suggests that they will be treated with respect:

> *"I need your help with something." or "Can you help me with something?"*

Some people who have attended my workshops have wondered if asking for the person's help is too "soft" and non-direct and doesn't indicate any degree of punishment for breaking an agreement. The truth is that you do actually need this person's help in order to resolve the situation. They must listen to your concerns, acknowledge the broken agreement, act reasonably to correct the problematic behavior, and sometimes apologize if necessary. The goal of this conversation is getting the person to align their behavior rather than continuing to rationalize or deny the broken agreement. You will need their cooperation in order to get to that point – that is why you ask for their help.

Part 2

Ask for the time you need to address this with them, and if now is not the best time to discuss it, schedule a time, ideally the same day, to discuss it:

"Do you have a few minutes?" or *"Is this a good time to talk?"*

Asking for just a few minutes of their time helps in a few ways. You are there to discuss a broken agreement, which is a failure, whether small or large, on their part. No one likes to be told they failed at something; no one likes criticism or feeling like they are being reprimanded, especially grown adults. This is why many people rationalize their behavior or deny wrongdoing. Once you state the broken agreement, the person may be inclined to become defensive of their actions, and now you are on opposing sides of an issue instead of working together for a solution.

While the goal of asking for their help in Part 1 of the Broken Agreement Script is to disarm and establish that you are working together, the goal of gaining a small time commitment from them in the second part is to keep them engaged in the conversation, let them know you intend to get right to the point, and lessen the possibility of them trying to postpone the conversation after they learn the topic you want to discuss. You are letting them know this doesn't have to be a long drawn-out conversation, and since they already committed a few minutes of their time, addressing this is the easiest path to putting it behind them.

Part 3

State the agreement and the current behavior that is out of alignment with the agreement. This addresses the cognitive dissonance that they are most likely already feeling, assuming they are aware of the broken agreement. Be concise and keep it factual.

If you lead with emotion, they will respond with emotion, and then your goal of simply fixing the situation or correcting the misaligned behavior will be usurped by an emotional urge to punish, which is inappropriate in a business setting, detrimental to the relationship in a personal setting, and not helpful in any situation.

Here are a few examples of stating the agreement and the misaligned behavior:

"We agreed that you would submit this to me by the 12th. Today is the 13th, and I have not heard from you."

"We have a value of respect, and you disrespected someone's idea in the meeting."

Stating facts keeps judgment and emotion out of the discussion and lets the other person know that this situation is fixable and can be handled maturely and calmly. Notice there are two things missing in each of these examples.

1. Don't discuss *impact*. In the first example in the previous list, adding the impact of the broken agreement would sound like this:

    "We agreed that you would submit this to me by the 12th. Today is the 13th and I have not heard from you. The rest of our timeline is tightened now for the other team members."

You may be tempted to tell the person the problem their behavior has caused due to frustration or other emotion, or you might feel the desire to punish them. However, declaring the severity of the impact gives the impression that it is okay to break an agreement that has a lesser impact than the one in question, when in fact any agreement that your company supports should be adhered to by its employees. There should be a business reason for an agreement to be in place that work should be done in a certain way. If that agreement is broken, there will surely be some degree of impact on the business. If there is no impact, then you are wasting company resources by having arbitrary rules and policies. When you need to address a broken agreement, leave out the impact because it is not helpful. Usually the damage is already done, and they are already punishing themselves through cognitive dissonance. Leaving out the impact will have the added benefit of making a difficult conversation easier.

- Don't use *ultimatums*. Adding an if-then ultimatum to our first example would sound like this:

  "We agreed that you would submit this to me by the 12th. Today is the 13th, and I have not heard from you. If I don't have it by the end of today, we will discuss if you can continue on this project or not."

Addressing this broken agreement should have the goal of giving the other person the chance to repair your trust and to give you the confidence that this will not happen again in the future, simply by cooperating with the agreement going forward. Ultimatums make people defensive and often devolve into a power play by the person issuing them. Simply by addressing the broken agreement, it is already implied that there will be consequences if it is broken again. Stating them at this time is usually an expression of emotion, which should be left out of this process.

Part 4

Ask for their help in solving the problem and then be silent and allow them to answer. You can use one of these prompts or create one that matches your own style:

"What should we do?"

"Can you help me out?"

"Can you help me understand?"

"I would appreciate any help you could give me."

"How should we handle this moving forward?"

"How do we fix this?"

Remember, there are three ways that people normally respond to cognitive dissonance: align, rationalize, or deny. At this point you should be able to expect the person to cooperate and agree to align the behavior in the future. If the person responds with excuses in the form of rationalization or denial, be ready to cite where and when the original agreement was made. If they deny that they knew about it before this interaction, be ready to move on by asking for understanding of the agreement at this time and for compliance in the future. This way you can at least establish this time as when they officially know about the original agreement, and you can base future interactions on it.

Their answer to your request for help in solving the problem will most likely reveal the reason they broke the agreement in the first place. The problem is usually in either desire or competence. Do they lack the desire to cooperate with company policy? Or do they not know how to complete the task? Do they need encouragement to get on board with the culture of the organization, or technical instruction to do the job satisfactorily? That will tell you how to direct the coaching they need to comply with company policies and procedures in the future, or if they are indeed not a good fit for your organization.

This is a decision point for the person. If they recognize your expectation of compliance with an agreement as a condition of the relationship continuing, then they will have to choose whether to align and continue the relationship, or to ignore the agreement and risk ruining the relationship. If they choose not to abide by the agreement and therefore risk ruining the relationship, it is a choice that they have made themselves, and the responsibility will be theirs. In that case, you can choose to limit business (or personal) dealings with this person and use caution when exchanging facts with them, or simply revert to Level One Maturity, in order to avoid future problems.

When addressing someone's behavior or actions that are misaligned with organizational or societal norms, it is best to be prepared for negative reactions that might result. If someone responds by shouting, it will create a hostile environment. Your first response should be that if you cannot discuss the problem without shouting then you will assume without discussion that they are no longer a good fit for the organization. If they respond by counterattacking your behavior or discussing anything other than the broken agreement at hand, they are sidetracking. Your response should be to tell them you are willing to discuss any other concerns they have after the current matter has been addressed. If they respond with unreasonable emotion like crying or saying "I've never done anything right in my whole life!" that may be beyond the scope of appropriate interaction for your relationship, and you should respond by suggesting that they talk to someone who can help with that, but you need to leave this conversation with the confidence that the problem won't happen again.

A bonus benefit of learning this skill is that you start to anticipate some situations where broken agreements happen, and you get better at *making* agreements so you can reduce the opportunity for there to be a broken agreement in the first place. I have coached salespeople on making better initial agreements with their clients so that there is a reduced incidence of breaking them later. For example, a salesperson should check in with a client and say something like "for us to meet your requested timeline of three months on this project we will need these things from you in the next two weeks. Will you be able to provide those things within that time?" This is trying to prevent broken agreements before they happen. If all parties agree to specific items like this, then there is less chance that someone will need to be held accountable later.

Broken Agreement Examples

Here are just a few real-world examples from my clients of broken agreements that were addressed using this script:

- Your client paid only a portion of your invoice with no request for extended payment terms.

- You were told you would receive a bonus check for $500, but the check you received was for $250.

- You gave approval for the implementation of a project, and a different project was implemented instead.

- Your boss said you would be the lead on a project and then announced someone else as the lead during a group meeting.

- A colleague promised you something by Tuesday, and it's now Wednesday, and you haven't received it yet, which pushes back your next deadline.

- An employee is not following the company dress code.

- An employee has been pursuing a personal side business during work hours.

- The head of a work team is giving special treatment to a select few employees who agree with her on political matters.

- Someone in the department frequently brings up controversial topics in the office.

- Someone in the office has loud phone calls, distracting others.

- Someone is not following breakroom rules.

Using the Broken Agreement Script in situations like these gives you a direct way to approach the broken agreement and begin communicating without emotion so that it can be discussed openly, and expectations can be clarified for the future.

Conditions for Addressing a Broken Agreement

The way you address any relationship problem will often determine your chances of success at resolving the problem.

> Addressing a problem quickly, privately, and with self-control is often critical to resolving the problem.

- **Timeliness matters.** Compiling a long list of offenses or letting the relevance of a broken agreement pass and bringing it up later is not helpful if you are trying to change the behavior or fix the relationship. If there is unacceptable behavior in the relationship, then address it right away so that you aren't letting resentment or discontent grow on your part, or letting the other person continue thinking their behavior is acceptable.

- **Privacy matters.** Maintaining privacy is critical to preserving respect and trust in the relationship. Addressing a relationship problem, especially a broken agreement, in front of other people will put the person on defense and cause them to lose trust in you. They will be inclined to protect their ego and defend their actions, and it will most likely affect the response and level of cooperation you get. If this happens, you may lose your opportunity to resolve the issue at all. Additionally, they may have an explanation for their actions that you did not expect, and they may need your help or instruction. Keep the discussion between the two of you in order to preserve respect and trust so that the relationship has a chance to continue in a healthy way once this broken agreement is resolved. If a coworker wants to bond with you by discussing a relationship problem they are having with someone else, but they do not intend to actually address or resolve the problem, discourage this by not participating. This creates a culture of gossip that will interfere with building meaningful relationships and will inhibit engagement and productivity.

- **Self-control matters.** If you let emotion get in the way and you attack the other person, you probably will not get far into resolving the problem. You will immediately put the other person on the defensive side, and *you* will have something to apologize for if you attack. Your resulting conversation will have more to do with your attack or outburst than it will with the actual problem. Remember, this could be something that the other person has tried to avoid discussing. By attacking them you allow them to focus on your poor choice of words instead of the issue at hand, which will only get in the way of resolving the problem.

A Dead Moose: A Problem You Can't Ignore

Plenty of relationship problems do not involve explicit broken agreements but require sensitive conversations. When was the last time you were on the receiving end of passive-aggressive behavior, the silent treatment, or playing games at any of the Levels of Maturity? In my workshops we call this type of problem a Dead Moose because it's something big and stinky that you cannot ignore.

These sensitive issues often go unaddressed for several reasons. Perhaps you have allowed it to go unaddressed because discussing it makes you vulnerable and could potentially be more painful than pretending not to notice the problem in the first place. Perhaps you fear that the other person will walk away from the relationship if you confront them about it. Perhaps you anticipate denial or backlash, or you doubt your communication skills at putting your feelings into words, or perhaps you just choose to avoid conflict at any cost. Many times, the signals of a problem are subtle, and you don't want to invent problems that don't really exist, so you let it go for some time hoping that it was all in your head. However, usually the more this "signal" behavior is ignored, the more it continues, meaning that the person is actually trying to tell you something, or invoke a response from you, or get you to ask what's going on, and this will continue until you address it or until it destroys the relationship. If you want to save the relationship, it has to be addressed and, just as with clearer broken agreements, the way you address the problem will often determine your success at resolving the problem. Timeliness, privacy, and self-control are critical.

A Dead Moose is not like a fine wine; it does not get better with age. In fact, it festers and begins to rot the things around it if you let too much time go by. If you have a Dead Moose, address it privately as soon as possible with the other person. The conversation is not going to get easier to approach as more time passes.

If you are truly interested in fixing the relationship problem, check your ego at the door before having this conversation. Sometimes our ego tells us to be confrontational in a *they offended me; I'm going to offend them back* way. If you have an *I just want them to know that I know what they're doing* attitude, all you will accomplish is disrespecting them. Trying to gain the upper hand in the relationship is not a solution to your problem, it's just an additional relationship problem because it introduces competition. Often when I'm coaching people on this, I'll ask them,

"What do you want the outcome or solution to this problem to be?" This question can help them articulate the problem in Part 3 of the Broken Agreement Script and they can end the conversation with an action item like "Let's handle this differently in the future," or "I would appreciate it if you talk to me directly if something is bothering you." The goal of this should not be just to "win" or to make the other person feel like they got caught doing something wrong; the goal should be to create a better relationship moving forward and to try to avoid having the same problem again.

A Dead Moose must be addressed with two goals in mind: to be able to continue the relationship after the problem is resolved, and to maintain respect for the other person throughout the discussion. If these are not your goals and you don't care to continue the relationship, then you are basically approaching your conversation as an opportunity to air your grievances before you end the relationship, and no script will help you fix it. Finding the right words to address relationship failures respectfully with the goal of fixing the problem and continuing the relationship can require patience and self-control (so you don't lose your temper), humility (so you can accept a genuine apology or explanation of circumstances), and commitment (so you can work together to fix the problem).

Even though it might not involve an explicit broken agreement, this type of relationship problem can usually be interpreted as a broken assumed agreement, as in assuming the kind of treatment we expect from each other when we have a friendly or working relationship, and so the Broken Agreement Script is very helpful here with a slight alteration.

In Part 3, instead of stating the agreement and the behavior that broke the agreement, say, "I'm sensing that . . ." and say what you have been noticing in the relationship. Preface it with a statement like "I could be way off base here, but I'm sensing that . . ." It would sound like this:

> *"Hi Fran, I need your help with something. Do you have a few minutes to talk? I could be way off base here, but I'm sensing that things have been different between us for the past few days, and I don't know why. Is there anything going on that I don't know about?"*

This will establish targeted communication about the issue at hand, make it easy for them to discuss it, and ideally you will learn what is bothering the person. Alignment and rationalization are not typical responses to a conversation starter like this. You will more likely either get an answer to your question and an honest discussion, or you may get a denial of the problem. You can't force someone to talk about a problem that they do not want to discuss, but you can make the person aware that you know something is going on and that you are not comfortable with it. If they deny that there is a problem and this is a person you have to work with, identify which of the Five Levels of Maturity the person is operating at and revert to that level in order to limit drama with them. For example, you may have to revert to Level One with this person and just say hello and goodbye politely or deal strictly with the factual exchange of information necessary for work matters. At this point, I like to leave the door open to discuss it in the future by saying something like "If you ever have a problem or are uncomfortable for any reason, please discuss it with me."

If this is a family member, the talk will be more difficult. Again, identify which Level of Maturity the person is capable of with you and revert there. You can hope to rebuild the relationship over time, but forcing a relationship that the other person does not want or cannot handle well will not work.

Remember from Chapter 3 that relationships work when both people are getting their needs met. If either one of you is not interested in meeting the other's need for a respectful and pleasant relationship free of emotional drama, then the relationship cannot continue as it is. Revert to Level One and seek to move on to Level Two and Three as time and circumstances allow. You may never get to a Level Five relationship with this person if they are prone to emotional games like silent treatment, passive-aggressive behavior, competition in the relationship, or even unspoken hostility toward you that you can sense when you are together.

These reminders can be applied to any relationship problem that you are interested in fixing.

Reminders for Addressing a Relationship Problem

Here's a cheat sheet for addressing a relationship problem:

- Address problems quickly – don't let too much time go by.
- Address problems privately so that your discussion can be candid and honest.
- Address problems with self-control of your emotions so that you don't attack the person.
- Strive to fix the problem, not punish the person.
- Always maintain respect throughout the discussion.

We certainly need these reminders for dealing with our more difficult, tedious, or distant relationships. However, when a problem or conflict arises with someone who is very important to us, these things might come more naturally because we genuinely want to keep these people in our lives, and we naturally care about our relationship with them and want to fix a problem when it arises. This is evidence that our motives matter when we address conflict. Your motives should always include maintaining respect for someone as a person, as well as controlling your ego while resolving the problem.

Serial Broken Agreements

There is a second type of Dead Moose that leaders have to be able to handle. It is when you have addressed a broken agreement with someone, used the Broken Agreement Script, and gained a reasonable promise of alignment, yet the broken agreement continues, or they continue to break different agreements. This problem is not about a specific agreement, it's about the relationship. Whether or not the relationship is contentious, they are refusing to align with their agreements. I call that serial broken agreements.

Often when someone acts this way it's because they feel like a prisoner in their current situation and they are trying to send a message that something is not okay. At that point you have to ask them about their desire for the relationship. Use the same variation of the Broken Agreement Script described earlier. It might sound like this:

> *"Hi Mike, I need your help with something. I'm sensing that every-thing is not okay between us. Do you sense that as well?"*

If Mike says, "Yes, we have a problem," then you can address the relationship problem. If Mike says, "No, everything is fine," then you can point to the broken agreements as evidence that everything is not okay. Regardless of Mike's answer, your next question should be:

"Do you want this relationship to be successful?"

If Mike's answer to that question is "Yes, I do," then say:

"Our relationship cannot be successful with broken agreements. Can I have confidence moving forward that our agreements will be honored?"

You have discussed the broken agreements before without resolution. If you want to rescue the relationship, you have to bring the relationship to the forefront of the discussion. Ask Mike what he needs from the relationship so you can work together successfully. If this radical commitment to saving the relationship does not work, then it is time to separate.

Unfortunately, there are times when someone's behavior leaves no other option than to let them go. They would rather leave it to someone else to fix their problems for them than to do it themselves, which may be difficult and require extreme courage. One of my clients had to let someone go due to continued diversion from company policies. When informed of their dismissal the employee said, "I didn't want to work here anymore anyway." My question then was "Well, why didn't they either quit the job when they decided it wasn't right for them anymore, or at least make sure they followed company policies until they got another job so they wouldn't get fired? Why did they make their employer decide for them?"

Stories of serial broken agreements from my clients highlight how it usually affects others in the organization. An employee could simply be trying to avoid work, which leads to extra work for someone else, or they may have more resentful intentions as in *I'm not happy here so I'm going to be spiteful and not comply with what is expected of me and make everyone else pay for my unhappiness until they do something about it and finally end this for me, rather than doing the mature thing of tackling my own problems myself.*

Either way it puts an unfair burden on those around them and leaders have to know how to address this behavior.

Playground Rules Don't Apply Here

If you let the behavior go it will likely continue, so if you have addressed a Dead Moose with a colleague and have not gotten a satisfactory result and it is affecting your ability to do your job well, then it's time to get a leader involved. Playground rules about not snitching on someone don't apply here because on the playground we weren't being paid. This is your career, and you can't spend this much time and have this much depending on a dysfunctional, hostile, or volatile environment.

At this point in one of my workshops I had a CEO stop me and say, "I don't know what Level Three is, but if I could get my entire organization to be good at Levels One and Two, do you know how much more money we could make?"

Level Two Quick Reference Guide

Success at Level Two Maturity is exchanging facts and information efficiently, keeping facts in context without misrepresenting or twisting them, answering questions earnestly, and honoring the agreements that we make. When we decide to follow through on all our commitments and agreements regardless of whether or not someone can hold us accountable for them, we're demonstrating the basic level of maturity and trustworthiness necessary for commerce to take place, and that's success at Level Two.

Failure at Level Two Maturity is arguing facts just to be difficult, twisting facts to mislead, and not doing what we agreed to do.

How to proceed with the relationship if someone fails at Level Two Maturity: If someone fails at Level Two interactions and this is not an essential relationship, revert to only Level One interactions. If the relationship must find a path forward, limit factual exchanges to necessity only, and use the Broken Agreement Script to hold them accountable for their agreements and address sensitive relationship issues. If you use the script with the right motives of fixing the relationship problem and maintaining respect for the other person, and you address broken agreements privately, in a timely manner, and with self-control over emotions, you can attend to these issues without damaging the relationship.

Skill learned: Use the Broken Agreement Script to hold people accountable for their agreements, including implied agreements, or to address sensitive relationship issues.

Level Three: Navigating Differing Opinions

W e don't have to agree on everything for us to have a successful relationship. In fact, we will rarely meet someone who agrees with 100% of our opinions.

Success at Level Three starts with being mature enough to be willing to see the world from a perspective that is different from your own and respecting the rights and boundaries of others even if you disagree with their opinion. Sometimes this is easier said than done, however, which is why it requires maturity and commitments such as these:

- I understand that everyone has the right to their own opinions.

- If I disagree with someone's opinion, I can still respect them as a person.

- If I disagree with someone important to me on an important issue, I will seek to understand their opinion and to explain my opinion to them, and to discuss how this might impact our relationship.

Success at Level Three Maturity is respecting others' rights and boundaries even when we disagree with their opinions, knowing when to avoid opinion-heavy topics, and building a business case to support our opinions in business.

Opinions can be controversial and fraught with emotion. We develop them based on the experiences we have had and the information we have accumulated until this point in life. You might have an opinion today that is different from the one you held five years ago because you have had more experiences, or you have more information on the topic today than you did then. When differing opinions come up in a relationship and we take the time to discuss what led us to those opinions, it can be a great relationship-building conversation because you are simply learning about the experiences that person has had up until now. This is an expression of respect for the other person, and, as we discussed in Chapter 2, it's doing something you don't have to do for someone, which is the way to build trust in your relationship. This sounds easy until the ego gets involved.

If I say that I liked a movie but you didn't like that movie, it probably wouldn't be that big a deal between us. However, just as in Level One and Level Two, if I'm angry with you over something else or if my ego is threatened at the time, I might take that opportunity to make you feel foolish for holding that opinion so that I can feel superior to you in some way or make you feel bad in some way, especially if there are others around who agree with my opinion instead of yours. That way I can make you feel ostracized over something as simple as a movie preference, which makes me powerful.

In a predictable age-based example, a client told me about his fifth-grade daughter whose school lunch table discussion was about different foods and how gross they are – sounds very fifth grade, right? When someone mentioned guacamole, his daughter said, "I like guacamole!" Another girl at the table decided that no one should speak to his daughter that week because she likes guacamole. She used his daughter's opinion to put her down and to show how powerful she was and that she could get the other kids to go along with ostracizing someone when she told them to, even if it was based on something as simple as a food preference. That was a tough week for the young girl, who was very cautious about sharing her opinions for a while, especially in the presence of someone who used her opinion to bolster their own ego. This is an easy example of failure at Level Three. We may not have the maturity to handle our differences with care in middle school and not use them against each other, but unfortunately it doesn't stop there.

One client told a story about Sarah and Joyce, who weren't getting along. Sarah suggested a seafood restaurant for their team lunch meeting and did not invite Joyce. When Joyce found out they went out without her, Sarah gave this excuse: "Oh last week you said you don't like seafood so I didn't think you would want to come." Sarah used her knowledge of Joyce's restaurant opinion against her to try to validate excluding Joyce from the meeting.

After several similar episodes, this company hired me to deliver relationships workshops for their teams. Sarah had failed at Level Three Maturity many times. The people she works with (and, I would venture to guess, people in her personal life as well) had figured this out and had pulled back to Level One and Two interactions with Sarah whenever possible. This interfered with her relationships and stopped people from getting too close so that they wouldn't get burned again by her. Until Sarah can move on to Level Three Maturity or beyond and prove that she can treat people respectfully and not use their opinions against them, she will most likely continue to form adversarial relationships in which trust is low and suspicions are high. Additionally,

Sarah's boss knows that Sarah cannot be trusted to interact at Level Three Maturity, so her future career will be affected by that as well. Not surprisingly, Sarah did not last very long at this company, which included integrity and respect as core corporate values.

Just like everything else, the degree to which differing opinions can be a jugular relationship issue correlates with the importance of the topic, as well as whether the differing opinions are respected or disrespected. Topics that are divisive and opinion-heavy should not be discussed in business. Even if you can discuss politics and religion without devolving into name-calling, it is unlikely that you will find all the people in your office on the same wavelength, and therefore it is best to avoid these types of discussions when business should be discussed instead. Discussions like this make it more difficult for people to show respect to each other, and they give ammunition to people who are inclined to play games at all the maturity levels.

Differing Opinions on Business Strategy: Build a Business Case

My clients have reported examples like this of Level Three failures in business in both petty office politics and also important business matters. The nature of opinions is that most of the time there is not an objective outcome, or a right answer. If I ask you what your favorite movie is, there is no right or wrong answer, and I don't need to try to convince you to like mine instead. However, there are more important matters on which our opinions may differ but a decision has to be reached, such as business strategy decisions.

Let's say you are in a strategy meeting and a decision needs to be made. You and another colleague have presented two opposite opinions on what the company should do. How will this decision be made? This depends on the maturity level of the people in charge.

Many times, in business, just like in middle school, the criteria someone uses for how the decision will be made are the criteria that will make them win. They will start a game that you are guaranteed to lose so that you will bow out and not even try to compete with them. If they have been there longer, they might say, "I've been here 10 years and you've been here 2 years, so just based on my experience at the company we should go with my solution." Or they might use position to outrank you: "I'm a vice president, and you are a frontline manager, so my solution is going to be better." Or they might use politics: "I know the CEO really well and I know she agrees with me on this." Or they might use education level: "I have a master's degree, so I know what I'm talking about here." In any of these scenarios their "my way or the highway" mentality is going to win, not because their idea is better than yours, but because they have been there longer, they outrank you, or they know someone important who could threaten your job. They chose criteria by which they know they can win, and therefore their opinion wins. That's the ego getting involved and manipulating the outcome, and this is a failure at Level Three.

Bob's legacy is a perfect example of this. A client in the heavy machinery industry was reviewing processes in place after Bob, a department manager at the plant, left the company. Every time my client asked a worker why something was done a certain way, they answered, "Because Bob said so." The procedures were inconsistent and sometimes redundant, but the department seemed to run on the mantra "Bob's way or the highway," and Bob fired or disciplined anyone who challenged his opinion on how things should be done. The client hired me to teach all the managers how to form and support their ideas and opinions by building a business case based on company data and the customer's best interest, so that next time a "Bob" came up with a procedure, there was a good business reason for it.

The way to make business decisions objectively is to build a solid business case for each opinion. The first premise of building a business case is knowing who your customer is and why they do business with you. Customers spend their money with your company for three reasons. I will use buying a suit as an example:

- Customers save *time* by hiring you to provide products or services for them, rather than creating those products or performing those services themselves. *If I tried to make a suit myself, it would take me a lot of time to learn how to do it and to design and create a suit.*

- Customers get a better *quality* of products or services by hiring you as an expert than they would if they created those products or services themselves. *If I made a suit myself, it would be a terrible-looking suit, so I get a better-quality suit by buying it from a clothing company rather than making it myself.*

- Given competition in the marketplace, customers get better *value* for their money by hiring you than by hiring someone else, so you should know where you fit into the marketplace of your products or services. This is usually due to the intersection of price and quality. We want to save time and get better quality than if we did it ourselves. *If I buy a higher-quality suit it should last longer and look better than if I buy a lesser-quality suit, which may be less expensive, so then I have to make a purchasing decision depending on how much quality I can get for what price I can pay in this category of product or service.*

Time, quality, and value are the three things that drive customers to delegate and buy products or services from you rather than doing it themselves or hiring your competition.

Once we understand that every business decision should be made based on time, quality, and value, then the answer to "How will we make this decision?" should never be based on tenure, position, or politics. This takes "you and me" out of the way. It's not my way or your way that wins; it's the best way for the business, which means the best way for our customer. If we disagree on how the company should proceed, then it's time to roll up our sleeves and get to work. Let's build a business case. Map out the problem, calculate the cost of having that problem, and talk about our options for solutions and the cost of those solutions. We can then calculate a return on investment for each solution based on real numbers, and we can try it in practice your way and my way and figure out which way performs the best for the customer and for the profitability of the business, and which one is safer, faster, more consistent, more secure, more reliable, and we have a winner! The winning solution should serve our customers best by saving them time, providing better quality, or providing the most value for their money.

If we make business decisions this way, an intern could possibly have a business idea that wins over a manager. This is the only way to harness ideas and talent from across all levels of the company. If we let egos get in the way and we base decisions on tenure and position, then only the top level of the company will ever be heard. The talent and knowledge at the lower levels of the organization, who frequently have more customer contact, and sometimes more energy and enthusiasm, than the top level, will be wasted.

One client told me a story of how a grassroots idea saved the company millions of dollars. This food industry customer built a large manufacturing plant, which was finished except for the rooftop air conditioning unit that was backordered for three months and put the whole job behind schedule. The plant could not run without air conditioning due to food safety issues.

Every hour that the plant was not operational meant a loss of over $50,000 in revenue to the client. If they were to wait for the full backorder period, this would mean a loss of over $45 million in revenue for the company. Of all the ideas that were analyzed, a salesperson suggested offering $5 million to the next-in-line air conditioning customer to trade places with them on the waiting list so that they could get their unit faster. At first, the management of the company scoffed at the idea of an unforeseen capital layout like that. But the salesperson put together a business case comparing all the costs, their idea was presented and approved, the other customer accepted, and as a result the manufacturing plant was up and running nine weeks faster than it would have been if they had waited and not taken such unconventional methods to solve the problem.

I have another client whose business depends on thousands of small transactions every day. They are famous for process-mapping the smallest details of their systems since saving a second on each transaction adds up to increased profits for them. If a process improvement is suggested, management's response is "Go get the data!" Regardless of who suggests it, a business case is required to support any changes made to the system because nothing in their business is based on opinion; there is plenty of data on which to base every decision.

One time a client asked me how to choose colors for a new product when their creative team could not agree. It was difficult for them to build a quantifiable business case for a creative choice like color when there is no clear right and wrong answer and, they thought, no way to monetize it. My answer was that all of their creative ideas exist to serve their customers, so send out the final choices to a focus group of their largest customers and see what they like! Their customers chose one of the colors by a wide margin, which made the decision a no-brainer. Take "you and me" out of the running so that we can be objective in our decisions and not let our egos get in the way. In business we can take every difference of opinion and turn to the customer we are supposed to serve and build the business case based on their best interest, even if there is not a traditional monetization of the issue. The problem is that takes a lot of work and instead of doing that work, some people want to rest on their seniority or their political contacts or their positional power so they can win. Then they wonder why morale and engagement and productivity aren't where they need to be.

Success at Level Three Maturity in business is considering opinions based on a business case, not the ego of the people involved. We need to know that every decision being made in the business is in the best interest of the customer and our business, not to boost the ego of any one person, no matter how high up on the company ladder they are. If a business case that considers speed, quality, return on investment, and customer feedback is presented, then that idea will gain support and the confidence of the organization, and experience less resistance than a "my way or the highway" approach. This confidence drives positive trends in engagement, morale, productivity, innovation, and retention, and is an effective and sustainable way to make business decisions.

Think of the buy-in that comes from having a business case behind a new initiative. When your staff asks why you're doing this, saying "because I said so" is going to drive a different level of engagement from them than saying "because the customer is choosing it over every other option, and we exist for the customer, and if we stop serving the customer we go out of business."

When Business Case and Mission Clash

For most businesses, in most instances, a business case investigates and reports on important stats like cost of deliverables, cost of labor time, opportunity cost, and ROI, which are measurable financial projections or results. But there are certainly times when adhering to or furthering the company's mission should eclipse the bottom line. A business case determining the best financial outcome should still be presented, but an informed decision can sometimes be made to override the financial win in favor of the mission. Even then the business case is still a vital part of the decision process because corporate spending on mission-related activities (usually charitable causes) has to be tracked and budgeted so that it does not weaken the sustainability of the organization.

Interestingly, most large organizations include a social responsibility statement in their mission and their customers are aware of it. The social responsibility policies that a corporation adopts usually appeal to their customer base in a way that benefits their bottom line anyway. For example, a restaurant that sponsors a local little league team enjoys community goodwill from that sponsorship, and they hope to be chosen by patrons over another restaurant in town because of it. This is a small example of how company mission and bottom line are usually inextricably connected, so that occasions where business case and mission clash are usually only in the short term.

Level Three Quick Reference Guide

Success at Level Three Maturity comes when we respect others even when we disagree with their opinions, know when to avoid opinion-heavy topics, use serving the customer as the barometer for making decisions (instead of using opinions), and build a business case to support our opinions in business.

Failure at Level Three Maturity includes mocking, disparaging, or shaming someone because of their opinion. Failure also includes adopting someone's opinion based on office politics, longevity at the company, nepotism, title, level of education, popularity, office bullying, or any other reason besides that it best serves the customer.

How to proceed with the relationship if someone fails at Level Three Maturity: If someone fails at Level Three interactions, revert to Level Two interactions if possible. Sharing personal opinions with someone is not required, and small talk can be managed when someone else is doing that. In a business solution setting, when opinions differ, always build a business case for your opinion based on the best interest of the customer, considering speed, quality, return on investment, and customer feedback.

Skill learned: Build a business case to support your opinion and ideas of how something should be done.

7

Level Four: Playing to Strengths and Working Around Weaknesses

No one likes to be criticized or have their weaknesses pointed out to them. Admitting mistakes and weaknesses is uncomfortable, and it puts the ego on high alert. The ego's job is to meet your needs, and the first need you have is to survive. In the animal kingdom, any weakness an animal has can be exploited by a predator, so being less than perfect makes us vulnerable to attack, and therefore weaknesses should be concealed in order to ensure your best chance of survival. While as modern humans we do not have daily encounters with predators in the wild who threaten our survival, the competitive spirit of the ego still drives some people to refuse to admit or show vulnerability so that they will be perceived as stronger or more powerful than someone else.

The problem is that if we cannot admit when we need help or input, then we cannot collaborate or work with anyone else. If we cannot admit when we make a mistake, then we cannot have fulfilling relationships. If we cannot consent to learn from the people around us or ask advice, then we will be stuck where we are and never grow in maturity. This is failure at Level Four.

If we are able to keep the ego under control and put aside the drive to be perceived as perfect, then we can collaborate and learn more than we can on our own. Collaboration requires understanding the premise that you and I know more together and can accomplish more together than we could if we each worked separately and kept our work from each other. Doing this means we have to listen to each other, share the credit for our work, build on each other's ideas, and allow our own ideas to be tweaked and improved. Collaboration does not happen without being vulnerable. It requires humility and caring about our outcome more than we care about being the smartest one in the room.

Success at Level Four is admitting mistakes, apologizing when necessary, concentrating on each other's strengths, working around each other's weaknesses, and providing feedback in a way that is sensitive to the vulnerability of others. Success at this level is what ignites gains in morale, engagement, and productivity.

Admitting Mistakes and Apologizing When Necessary

Projecting an image of perfection is a full-time job. You cannot simultaneously build relationships and feign perfection for any length of time. Many studies have been done about the necessity of vulnerability for human connection and healthy relationships; there is no need to get into that here except to state the overwhelming finding that someone who is unwilling to show vulnerability to another person will eventually wind up pushing that person away emotionally, rather than drawing them in, which may have been the original desire.

Many people have internalized their aversion to vulnerability without even realizing it, to such a degree that they have a very hard time apologizing even for an innocent mistake. Recently I was on a flight home after a speech and my suitcase was missing from the overhead compartment when we landed. I waited for everyone to get off the flight, and I took the last remaining small black suitcase and got in line at the information desk assuming that whoever owned that bag had taken mine instead. Sure enough a guy came running in with my suitcase. He was in such a hurry that he took my bag by mistake, got all the way to the parking garage before he realized it, and had to come running back inside. He saw that I had his bag, so he approached me directly. At this point his mistake had cost me about half an hour. I wanted to get home, I was annoyed at the wasted time, and I was concerned about whether or not I would get my bag back that night or if it would drag on for days until the airline found it.

However, anyone who travels a lot knows these things are not uncommon, so when I saw him with my bag, I was relieved that this was an easy one and it was over already. What should have been a simple exchange went south when he approached me and said, "You have my bag." He did not say, "I'm sorry I took your bag by mistake," or "Oh, I'm so happy to see my bag – sorry about the mix-up," or "Thank you for taking my bag to the information desk so we could work this out." Nope. He said, "You have my bag," indicating that I was responsible for this. I probably should have just traded the bags and not said a word since I know that there was no satisfaction to be had in this situation, and if he did not lead with an apology then I probably wasn't going to get one.

But I did not do that because by then I was mad. I said, "How did I get your bag?" and he said, "There was a mix-up on the plane." Are you kidding me – at this point, this guy was seriously not going to apologize? I said, "Well, I wasn't mixed up . . ." and he cursed at me, took his bag, and left without acknowledging that he cost me time or that I *saved* him an immense amount of time by taking his bag off the plane to the desk.

We were strangers. There was no competition between us. The situation was obvious that he took my bag by mistake and cost me time. There was no reason not to approach me, apologize, get his bag, and leave peacefully. The only reason that did not happen is because his ego was threatened by his honest mistake, because it meant that he isn't perfect, which perhaps is a lie he had been trying to tell himself or others. This guy could not apologize to a stranger for an insignificant honest mistake. If he had trouble in this situation, what is it like to be his co-worker, or his spouse, or his neighbor, or his employee, or his vendor?

Most of the time, admitting a mistake comes along with an apology. People are usually more willing to apologize for an insignificant mistake than they are for a more substantive mistake that has caused harm. For instance, it is usually easier for someone to apologize for saying something incorrectly, or for being a minute or two late, because they know that no significant harm was caused and they expect full absolution from the other person, which makes them feel good. In other words, they apologize for their own benefit, and they stand to gain moral points and a subsequent ego boost from their minor insignificant mistake because they took the moral high road of apologizing. Yet when more substantive harm has been caused, people are more reluctant to admit fault and apologize for the harm they have caused. They refuse to see themselves as someone who caused harm and must apologize for it. This is the ego getting in the way of the relationship again. They might feel that if they made a mistake and hurt you in some way that you could hold it against them, you might think they are no longer good enough to have a relationship with you, or you might think that you now have the upper hand in the relationship as they try to get back on your good side. Their ego is too fragile for those thoughts, so instead they just will not admit fault or will not apologize even when fault is obvious.

I have a small client in the entertainment industry who hired me for a leadership workshop for the whole company. There were about 60 people in the room. During the workshop an associate told a story about how the human resources department did not pay her for a month when she first started the job, and she had to use the Broken Agreement Script on them to fix the mistake. The problem was that the human resources department was one person, and she was in the room at the time. At the break, the HR employee approached the associate and said, "That story is not true, I have the records to prove it, and you made me look bad. Please recant the story in front of the group and admit that you were mistaken, and you owe me an apology for making me look bad." The associate refused to recant the story and refused to apologize. This became a standoff at the company, and the associate wound up quitting her job the next day. She quit her job rather than admit that she was wrong and apologize in front of the group.

Some people know they caused harm or hurt you in some way, but their ego will not let them apologize. Instead, they try to overcompensate and go out of their way to do or say something nice, or to speak nicely and charm you into a fun conversation, especially in front of other people. They do this to alleviate their own guilt. If they are able to engage with you, then they are satisfied that everything is okay in the relationship. If you insist on remaining hurt or angry, then you are the one with the problem, not them.

Succeeding at Level Four Maturity means not only offering a sincere apology when it is warranted, but also accepting a sincere apology graciously from someone else without holding it against them.

There are a few ingredients to a good apology:

- Acknowledge the mistake that was made.
- Express regret.
- Commit to not doing it again.
- Be sincere at each step.

If these ingredients are present, there is no excuse not to accept this sincere apology from someone and humbly let go of the mistake that was made. A good apology can put an end to all the games that the ego can start.

We succeed at Level Four when we can admit our mistakes and apologize for them, ask for help when we need it, admit when we do not know the answer to something, or admit that we have weaknesses. This does not diminish our worth; conversely, it will build the trust that other people have in us because – guess what – other people already know that we are not perfect. Being vulnerable in front of others does not mean that we have to overshare or go beyond what would be appropriate for the relationship and the situation, but it does mean that you can trust me, because if I make a mistake I will admit it, not blame it on something or someone else (including you), and I am willing to learn from you if the opportunity arises. It means that I do not consider myself to be superior to you, so I do not fear falling into inferiority next to you.

In other words, I am not competing with you, so I will not try to win in our relationship, and therefore you do not have to fear losing in our relationship. If I am successful at Level Four Maturity, then you have confidence that I view you as my equal, that neither of us is expected to be perfect, and that I will treat you as a person deserving of respect despite any mistakes or weaknesses. You can be confident that you can be less than perfect in front of me, and I will not use it against you to gain the upper hand in the relationship, or to hold it over your head in any way in our relationship.

Being Less Than Perfect

Here are some examples of things people say when they are willing to be less than perfect in front of others:

- "I'm sorry."
- "I was wrong."
- "I don't know the answer."
- "I made a mistake."
- "Will you help me?"
- "That's one of my weaknesses."

The Negativity Bias

Most species are wired always to be on the lookout for danger; anything suspicious in their environment is a potential threat to their survival. We have that instinct as well. Our peripheral vision is a perfect example of our built-in danger warning systems. It enables us to perceive motion and objects outside of our direct visual path so that our brains can instinctively evaluate them for potential threats. Our instincts are hyper-skewed toward survival and anything that might threaten it; hence, we notice, evaluate, and focus on negative factors more urgently and more thoroughly than positive factors.

Psychologists call it the *negativity bias*. It is the idea that negative factors will have a greater effect on our psychological state of mind than neutral or positive factors. We feel more impact from negative factors than we do from positive factors in matters of otherwise equal weight. The negativity bias overemphasizes the negative in an effort to heighten our awareness and protect ourselves. We are naturally highly sensitive to negativity in our surroundings because of this survival instinct. You walk through your home every day and probably do not stop to appreciate that all appliances are in working order, the plumbing is working, electricity is on, the house is at the right temperature, and the roof is not leaking. If any one of those things is not working properly it could certainly cause a big problem, so why aren't we as reactive in a positive way when everything is fine?

A simple example is online reviews of a product you consider buying. You've decided that you are interested in this product. The look and price of it are acceptable, the description seems on point for what you need, and now it's time to read reviews. Which people do you automatically think are on your side? You know it's the one-star reviewers! They are looking out for you. They purchased this product and got a raw deal. It broke, it did not work, it's flimsy, it's undersized, it's not worth your money. They do not want you to make the same mistake they did. Wow, they are true friends, thank God for those people. The people who left five-star reviews must be less intelligent if they could not see what is not perfect about this product, or they must be devious if they want you to fall into the same trap. Either way their opinion is less meaningful to you than the one-star ratings, which you view with your own protection in mind.

The negativity bias is evident if you do the math on online ratings. With a scale of one to five stars, an overall rating of 3.0 would be exactly average. However, one-, two-, and three-star ratings are considered to be "critical reviews," as in they criticize the product. Only four- and five-star ratings are considered "positive reviews." This is because consumers give more weight to the negative reviews than they do to the positive reviews. Furthermore, we expect to see full explanations of why something only merited four stars instead of five before we make a purchase.

Not only do we have this negativity bias in our nature, but it is reinforced by nurture as well. My parents had 12 children. My mom does not recall any teachers calling our house to discuss a good grade on a test or a well-behaved student; there was only enough time to address the problems. When report card time came, as long as everything looked acceptable, there wasn't much time given to it. Getting a D in chemistry or failing a math test received much more attention than any of the As and Bs that came through the door. The reality that negative behavior merits attention more urgently, and therefore more effectively, than positive behavior teaches many children from an early age to "act out" in order to get a busy parent's attention.

With nature and nurture reinforcing our negativity bias, and our ego always poised to ward off attack, it is not difficult to understand our tendency to notice negative factors more than positive factors in our environment, in ourselves, and also in other people. We notice other people's faults because it makes us feel that we have a better chance of survival. If you have ever played chess online, you may have noticed that every time your opponent makes a mistake, your calculated chance of winning increases. The negativity bias is instinctive because of our strong drive to survive. This can create a relationship barrier. If we are always pointing out other people's faults and thinking that if they have faults it ultimately benefits our chances of survival over theirs, then how do we form any good relationships at all?

Thankfully, even if we cannot help but notice negative things about other people, we have the ability to override the urge to point them out or dwell on them. We can act at Level Four Maturity, navigating our interactions with other people without exploiting their vulnerabilities, even though we may be aware of them. This is what we naturally want other people to do for us as well. You do not list your weaknesses on your résumé or online profile. You list your strengths and your accomplishments because you want people to know what your capabilities are; you want them to be impressed with you and to trust you. You want to be judged benevolently based on your accomplishments and your skills, not your weaknesses. We are each aware of our own weaknesses, and we do not want other people to concentrate on them all the time. If we want other people to view us benevolently and concentrate on our positive qualities, then we must do that for them also. This is what makes our good relationships work.

Concentrate on Strengths, Work Around Weaknesses

Americans spend a lot of time driving. In total we drive over three trillion miles in an average year.[1] Most people drive the same routes over and over again commuting to work or school or to see family. But what happens when you go from being the driver to being a passenger on one of these very familiar routes? You might suddenly notice a house or a landmark that you have never seen before. As a driver your eyes have to focus on the road, other cars, intersections, and hazards. If there is a house on the right at a busy intersection where you always turn left, you may never have noticed it before. Your focus is on the traffic coming through the intersection, waiting for your opportunity to turn. That house has always been there, you just never saw it before because you had to focus on the traffic ahead.

As a driver you narrowed your field of vision in a classic physiological response to a stressor or, in this case, the need to concentrate on the road. When you focused on one part of your surroundings, you could not see a different part. As a passenger, you can have a different perspective. You do not have to focus on the traffic for survival, and you can broaden your view and notice other things around you. This raises the interesting question of what determines which stimuli or factors in a given situation draw our focus and whether we can, in fact, consciously choose where to direct that.

Many psychology studies try to answer that question about focus. All you have to do is a quick internet search for studies on selective attention. The studies show that our brains work in amazing ways to filter out, either consciously or subconsciously, certain stimuli and information in our environment in order to focus on what is necessary for our current task, what is critical to our survival, what is of interest to us at that particular time, or what we are trying to accomplish. I sometimes conduct these experiments in my workshops to illustrate that the majority of people can be oblivious to an obvious stimulus in a situation where they are focusing on something else in the room. When I turn the experiments into a competition, it exaggerates the results even more because people are hyper-focused in order to win, and so even fewer of them notice the stimuli in question. When they are alerted to the previously ignored stimulus, people always laugh because it was so obvious.

Marketing and advertising firms get paid a lot of money to direct our focus in one direction or another. Any food product will promote its best features on the front of the label. When you see big red lettering that says, "Good Source of Vitamin C" or "Recommended Daily Amount of Fiber" or "Low in Saturated Fats," they are probably diverting your attention from the amount of calories, fat, sugar, sodium, carbohydrates, or anything else that might deter you from eating that product if you thought about it for too long. Clearly the manufacturers want to promote the strength of their product and ignore its weakness. If I decide to eat ice cream it's not because it's a "Good Source of Calcium," but seeing that on the carton might make me feel less guilty about eating it, which is exactly their goal. It's a classic marketing strategy: *Look at this, not that.*

When we concentrate on one thing, we often do not see something else that's happening around us. If people notice different things in a situation, it does not mean some people are smarter than others. It's all about what we prioritize to concentrate on, and that we, in fact, subconsciously choose that all the time, but we can decide to do it consciously as well.

This is what happens when you concentrate on someone's strengths. If you concentrate on someone's best traits, you simply aren't looking at their weaknesses. You're constantly reminding yourself of where they excel. It does not mean they do not have weaknesses. It means that you aren't looking for them all the time. You aren't always looking for opportunities to point out their faults. You manage their weaknesses by not convicting them for those weaknesses, and by concentrating instead on their strengths and on the role this person has in your life.

> Why is it easy for you to get along with some people and not others when everyone has weaknesses?

This is how your best relationships became easier, more natural, more rewarding than others. In your best relationships you already do this for the other person. Think of someone you enjoy spending time with. You do not enjoy this person because they're perfect. You know they aren't perfect, but you do not focus on their weaknesses; you focus on the things that make that person enjoyable to you.

Somehow that person built trust with you. Did they stick up for you, validate something you said in a group, agree with an idea you had, do something they did not have to do for you, empathize with you, or in some way demonstrate that they are acting in your best interest? Once you have that confidence in someone, there is a switch that you turn on for that person. It changes the way you see them. You see them as a friend, or an ally, and you view them more benevolently. You concentrate on their strengths. You are likely to describe them by their strengths, or their best qualities, when you are speaking about them. You tend to be more forgiving toward their weaknesses. You even use different words to describe the same personality traits, essentially turning what some people may see as a weakness into a strength. Think about how you would describe someone you like versus someone you do not like. If you like someone, you would say they are laid back or easygoing. If you do not like that person, they are lazy. If you like someone, they have a sophisticated or "dry" sense of humor. If you do not like them, they are sarcastic and arrogant. If you like someone, they are frugal. If you do not like them, they are cheap. Your friend is spontaneous and fun, versus impulsive and irresponsible. Your friend is passionate, versus opinionated. Either consciously or subconsciously, you have chosen to concentrate on this person's strengths because they have earned your confidence that they will work in your best interest and not compete against you.

In the relationships in our lives that we choose ourselves, like our spouse or our friends or the people we hire, concentrating on strengths should be easier and more natural because, after all, we chose this person to be in our lives. However, there are so many relationships in our lives that we do not choose, like family, colleagues, classmates, teachers, neighbors, and customers. There are probably more people in our lives that we did not choose than those we did choose. Whether or not you chose a person, you still have to make a decision. Will you concentrate on this person's strengths, talents, abilities, and endearing qualities, or will you spotlight their weaknesses, failures, and idiosyncrasies? In your best relationships you look benevolently at them, recognize their strengths, and work around their weaknesses. Succeeding in each relationship and ultimately getting along with the people around you depends on your choice of where to put your focus when you are with them. Your ability and decision to do this reflects your own maturity level because regardless of where you decide to focus, it will not eliminate the person's weaknesses. However, it can provide the opportunity to build trust, bring out their best performance and ideas if they feel respected, and set the relationship up for success. Relationships like that bring more fulfillment, peace, and happiness to our lives than low-trust relationships.

We have the ability to make more of our relationships successful by deciding to concentrate on the strengths and work around the weaknesses of the people around us.

This is not only an opportunity to look for the good in people, but also a valid business policy. I have heard many client stories of people who lost their jobs over a weakness that could easily have been managed. The reason they were hired is that they had a strength that would benefit the company in that job; losing them deprives the company of the value that strength brought to their job and imposes turnover costs as well.

A client told me about an important lesson they learned. Ann got hired at the company for her first job. She arrived every day ready to work and did her job well. Her branch office had a very social culture of chitchat around the water cooler and restaurant lunches. Ann was wary of participating, having been warned by other people of mixed experiences with office gossip and office politics. She said hello and goodbye to everyone, made minimal polite conversation, and did social things on her own time instead of the company's. Whether you consider this to be a weakness or a strength could depend on your own experience with office gossip. Ann's boss fired her because she did not "fit in with office culture," and the company wound up facing a wrongful termination suit. If her boss had focused on Ann's strength in her job performance and not on her lack of interest in office drama, which her boss saw as a weakness when team coherence was considered, everyone could have benefited, including the bottom line of the company. Her boss could have set up official team building time in order to bolster team coherence and make Ann and possibly others feel more comfortable about belonging while also maintaining professionalism.

Another client relies on their sales team for high-volume revenue-producing tasks every day, as do most organizations. Robert was their highest-grossing salesperson and was a big-picture guy. He hated details and was spending valuable time figuring out tedious reporting. He did the math and asked for an assistant to help him with support tasks so he could spend his time on sales, making both himself and the company much more money. His boss said, "We don't have assistants for salespeople. If we assign one for you, then we have to do it for everyone." Robert left and went to a company that gave him an assistant so he could concentrate on sales. The company lost their highest-grossing salesperson because of his weakness with tedious tasks. This could have been handled so many different ways. Didn't all the salespeople hate the reports? Could they be streamlined or simplified? Could there be two or three support people for the whole department who handled these tasks? Could he get training on how to organize his information to make it easier? His boss did not take the time to work around any of these strategies to fix the problem, and she let his weakness ruin the value he brought to the company.

Another client did a better job. Jennifer's job at the company was to manage live event production, and her perfectionism served her well and helped the company create excellent events for their customers. It's part of the job that things can go wrong at live events, and every little hiccup caused her stress and often led to an outburst at a colleague. There was a clear answer. Jennifer's job was not dependent on knowing every little hiccup and how it got fixed while the event was underway. My client thought about how to concentrate on Jennifer's strength and work around her weakness and decided that she did not have to be on radio communication with all other staff once an event started. She would only be made aware of problems that needed her attention. Jennifer was able to focus on her job and not be distracted by things that she did not have to fix, and everyone else was able to do their jobs without the added layer of stress of her micromanaging them. By managing her impulse to try to control everything at the event, which is impossible for one person, the company was able to benefit from Jennifer's event expertise and not face HR complaints afterward.

Ann showed prudence and restraint in staying away from office politics. Robert showed a high-performance drive to close sales without letting details get in the way. Jennifer showed perfectionism and the desire to control the details of a large project. All of these professionals have tendencies that could be seen as weaknesses or strengths depending on who is describing them and what the situation is. This is so true of all of us. Pessimism with a tendency toward paranoia would be a weakness if you apply for a job motivating and inspiring others. However, it might make you an excellent disaster preparedness expert or contingency planner. A suspicious nature might be a weakness if you are a professional athlete who has to trust your teammates, but it could be your greatest strength if you are a cyber security expert guarding your company against technology hacks, breaches, and internet viruses.

When an employee presents a true weakness that impedes them in their job responsibilities, there are ways to work around this too. For example, many people do not like delivering presentations. If this task is more than 10–15% of an employee's job and they have a true aversion to it, then they might want to consider a job change. However, if this comes up only occasionally, then this weakness can be managed like any other. Can you delegate it to someone else instead and have the two employees trade some responsibilities to make it fair? Can you get the employee some training on presentation skills to help them feel more comfortable? Can you assign a presentation partner so that the task can be shared, and the employee feels more comfortable? Can you change the setting of the presentation; for instance, let the employee sit at the table and talk instead of standing in front of the room? There are many things you can do as a manager to set your employee up for success and let their strengths shine while working around their weaknesses.

This is especially important in diverse and multigenerational teams. When people come from different backgrounds, it's very easy to obsess over differences. This is problematic if the ego and your survival instincts get involved and view differences as the other person's weakness. An older person might view a team member's youth as inexperience, while a younger person might think an older team member is out of touch with current market trends. A person born in a different country might think the other team members lack a global perspective, while someone else might think the foreigner is unfamiliar with domestic business principles. Concentrating on strengths instead might mean viewing these differences as valued perspective, experience, or potential for innovation that other people can bring to your ideas and products, or even simply concentrating on that person's individual talents and skills regardless of the ways they are different from you.

This also means leveraging strengths. Several people doing the exact same job next to each other is not a team. They become a team when the strengths of each person are leveraged for the good of the team, so that they can work cohesively to be better than they were individually and each person can say, "I'm not good at this; can you do it, and I'll do what I'm good at for all of us?" That is when teamwork is achieved through concentrating on strengths.

As with most leadership principles, leaders have to set this example from the top down in an organization in order for colleagues to do this for each other and have it become part of company culture. Many of my clients at one time or another have relied on personality style assessments in their human resources departments to identify strengths and work styles. Assessments like Myers Briggs, DiSC, True Colors, and CliftonStrengths are great tools for identifying and communicating your tendencies, comfort zones, habits, and the way you see the world. These assessments are designed to educate you on recognizing your own strengths and tendencies, and they encourage you to adjust your style to better work with other styles.

In my experience, the problem is that most people do not use them that way, and I have occasionally seen these assessments do more harm than good. They assume that people are at Level Five Maturity and ready to self-actualize and put other people's needs first in order to work well with others and make their colleagues' lives easier. More often, however, once people identify themselves as a certain style, they communicate that to their colleagues and have expectations that people will adapt to them in that way instead of the other way around. One client called me to say that after taking the assessments his team espoused their different styles and when one person stood his ground and expected others to change their approaches in order to work with him, the others all followed suit. Work effectively stopped while they were at a stand-off on who would humble themselves first to give in to the other people. We worked with the team on the Five Levels of Maturity, concentrating on strengths and working around weaknesses, and other topics in this book so they could return to productivity as a team.

Concentrating on strengths and working around weaknesses is a crucial skill for working, living, and getting along well with others. If you view others benevolently, it brings out the best in them, whether it's business performance or personal matters. For most people it inspires them to trust you and want to validate your benevolent treatment of them by living up to it, and to treat you benevolently in return.

Giving Positive and Corrective Feedback

The goal of giving any feedback should be to improve future performance. The way to do this is to reinforce the positive and to correct the negative. You must have both, given separately, in the moment when each is genuine. Because everyone has different strengths and weaknesses, everyone will need tailored feedback on the things they do well and the things they need to improve.

If you cannot work around a weakness, it will require corrective feedback to improve it. It is important to recognize that it takes courage and humility to accept criticism of one's performance in any job or relationship because it can hurt the ego. Level Four Maturity is required both to accept and to give corrective feedback in a constructive, healthy, and helpful way so that we can learn from it, and it can accomplish its goal of improving future performance.

Giving feedback that improves the performance of someone else is the number one most valuable skill in any leadership role. I am already responsible for succeeding in my own job performance, but if I can help improve the performance of the people on my team and they can be more successful in their roles because of my effectiveness at giving both positive and corrective feedback, then my value to the organization just multiplied by the number of people on my team. This one skill has the power to multiply my effectiveness as a manager.

The manager's job is to get every person on their team to perform as well as they can in their role. The skill that will get them there is giving effective feedback. If feedback is given the right way, it can be the difference between the employee succeeding and failing in their role. If the manager is as invested in their performance level as the employee is, and is hyper-focused on helping them by reinforcing the positive and correcting the negative, then the employee will be much more likely to succeed in their role.

It is the responsibility of the manager to consistently provide whatever feedback is necessary to get (or keep) team members on the right track to succeed. Raising the performance level of the team in this way is the reason to have a manager in the first place. If the team could perform at the same level *without* a manager, then the organization is wasting money by having the manager. I recently spoke to an employee at a company who said he likes his manager. When I asked why, he told me, "He leaves me alone and lets me work." Is the bar that low? Instead of raising their employees' performance level, there are managers out there actually preventing people from doing their jobs. They think it is their job to criticize, and they do it in a way that tears people down instead of setting them up for success.

Most managers recognize that corrective feedback is sometimes necessary, but some either do not go about it the right way, or at the right time, or they are uncomfortable giving the corrective feedback, so they avoid the situation all together, which allows subpar results to continue.

Common Feedback Pitfalls

There are two common pitfalls that people frequently fall into with feedback, and we will examine each of them here.

- Withholding positive feedback when it is due
- Confusing the message by using positive feedback to cushion the blow of negative feedback

Pitfall #1: Withholding Positive Feedback

Some people take a "no news from me is good news" approach and only address negative behaviors and mistakes, giving nothing but criticism, withholding all positive feedback.

In my experience, the reason most often cited by managers for refusing to give praise or positive feedback to their employees is the mindset that if people are praised, they will expect a raise to go along with it. This logic is flawed because it suggests that someone is hired to perform in an average capacity at their job, and if they do a great job they will get paid more. When an employee is hired to do a job, it should be expected that they will do the job as well as it can be done, to the best of their ability, for the agreed upon salary. There are associations and firms that collect data on what the average salary range is for positions in every industry in any location. That research should be done before an employee accepts a job offer. Accepting an offer should mean that the employee agrees to do the job to the best of their ability for that salary. They aren't being paid to do an okay job, and anything beyond that is rewarded by increased pay. If this is clear, then when they do the job successfully as expected, it can be acknowledged, reinforced, and even celebrated so that it is repeated.

While that may be the most often cited reason for withholding compliments on a job well done, I have also observed managers who deliberately withhold feedback that could have improved someone's performance because they want to be the most qualified person in the department. This is ego and competition getting in the way of doing business, and it certainly does not have the customer's best interest in mind.

This is also a common problem in personal relationships driven by ego, insecurity, and competition. People do not deliver compliments or praise to their friends, family, or significant other and instead only criticize because they want to feel superior to the other person, have the upper hand in the relationship, or hoard points against the other person for the future. Their ego is in control, and they are only looking for opportunities to criticize. This is usually an attempt to make themselves appear superior in some way, or to mask a perceived inferiority, and is usually born out of insecurity in the relationship. They are not working in the other person's best interest by withholding a well-deserved compliment, or other complimentary information that would benefit their friend. People who consistently criticize but never give positive feedback when it is due will only push people away eventually because we respond much better to positive reinforcement than we do to correction.

The tech industry has spent billions of dollars researching and developing positive reinforcement features on smartphones, video games, gambling machines, apps, and social media. Every trigger, vibration, customized tone and ring, virtual firework, buzz, level, badge, ding, and point scored is designed to create a dopamine release in response to a pleasurable experience. The more a user is inclined to go back to their product again and again to get a dopamine hit, the more it benefits the company's bottom line.

Dopamine is a powerful natural stimulant that embeds a memory of a positive response to a certain behavior. It is the brain's way of remembering a successful behavior that brought recognition and praise and should be repeated. When you pro-vide positive feedback to someone for a behavior, decision, idea, effort, kindness, joke, or job well done, it triggers a dopamine release and creates a desire to repeat that behavior. When you see a behavior from someone that you want to be repeated, positive feedback is the way to encourage that. Just like the home team benefits from homefield advantage because the stadium is full of fans screaming in support of the team, when we are recognized for a job well done, it motivates us to raise our performance level. The basic physiologic response to positive reinforcement, which is the release of dopamine, encourages someone to repeat behav-iors that are positively recognized or rewarded.

Positive feedback releases dopamine, which is the brain's way of remembering that this was a successful behavior, which brought recognition and praise, and should be repeated.

Positive feedback is a critical relationship builder because not only does it show the other person that you are working in their best interest and are therefore willing to give compliments and praise when it is due, but it also reveals which behaviors and actions you would like to see repeated in the relationship.

You are never going to raise someone's performance level to their highest potential or create a healthy relationship without providing positive feedback and encouragement along the way.

Pitfall #2: Confusing the Message

Some people try to soften the blow when corrective feedback is necessary by giving positive and corrective feedback together, which is confusing to the recipient and makes the positive feedback appear to be disingenuous.

Raising someone's performance level requires both reinforcing the positive and correcting the negative; doing it effectively means doing it separately. Many people feel uncomfortable giving corrective feedback because they know it is not pleasant for the person receiving it. They try to soften the blow by preceding it with positive feedback, praising one thing only to then criticize something else in the next breath. This is confusing to the recipient and makes the positive feedback appear to be disingenuous. It might appear like this:

- Manager basically ignores the employee's work output while everything is going well.

- Employee makes a mistake.
- Manager addresses the employee by saying they have been doing well with task A all along, but they made a mistake with task B, and it needs to be redone.

Why was the manager withholding the positive feedback that the person does a great job with task A? If the manager had previously told the employee that they're consistently doing a great job with task A when it was noticed, it would have proven that they're working in the employee's best interest. Instead, the manager has been holding back positive things to say about the employee until it benefited the manager by making it easier to give the employee corrective feedback. That's not in the employee's best interest; that's in *the manager's* best interest.

If it is only offered as a cushion before corrective feedback is given, then that kills the dopamine and negates the initial positive feedback you just gave. The recipient can usually sense there is a big "but" coming next, so they are not even fully absorbing your initial positive feedback, and they will not learn to repeat the positive behaviors that are being complimented as a cushion to the criticism that follows. They might already know what mistake or failure you are about to address, and they are bracing themselves to hear about it, or their mind is racing trying to figure out what the failure is that you are about to address. The opportunity to recognize behavior you want repeated, which is the intended goal of the positive feedback, was lost here.

If the only time someone hears positive feedback from you is to pave the way for corrective feedback, then it cannot be appreciated or trusted, and it can be dismissed as patronizing. The positive effect it may have had is destroyed by the corrective feedback right away.

Annual performance reviews are a prime example of this bad managerial habit. Most reviews usually start out giving vague approval of the overall job the employee is doing before the bulk of the time is spent on "opportunities for improvement." I remember every time a manager pointed out that I had an "opportunity for improvement" with more clarity than any category that was passed over with a "good job on that" type of dismissal.

Positive feedback should be given whenever it is due, not held until something negative occurs and a cushion is needed for the ease and comfort of the manager. There should be plenty of opportunities throughout the training process for sincere positive reinforcement and encouragement. Each time a manager notices a job well done, a good idea, or an extra effort, it should be acknowledged in the moment when the thought is genuine, and the timing is relevant for a dopamine release to be connected to the recent effort. More specific positive feedback is better than a vague *You're doing a good job lately*. Praise the specific action, decision, effort, or behavior so that it can be repeated. Thank the employee for doing a great job.

Giving positive feedback when it is sincere about what is working well builds a foundation of trust, lets the employee know you're working in their best interest, and puts all corrective feedback in perspective. Then when the situation arises that requires correction, you do not have to go on and on, softening the blow with positive feedback about something else. Make it short and to the point. It will be received better if you have been forthcoming with positive feedback before then. If this is handled well, nothing in a performance review should be new information. All positive and corrective feedback should have been given in the moment throughout the year, and nothing should be saved for review time. It should be a *review* of all the feedback that was already given during the year.

Separating positive and corrective feedback will make *both* more effective, more trusted, and more appreciated, and it will accomplish the goal of improving performance because the recipient can trust the authenticity behind each.

Giving Positive Feedback

Here are some tips for praising strengths generously:

- The goal is to release dopamine, so give positive feedback independently of other feedback.
- Be sincere. If you do not mean it, do not say it.
- Be specific. What actions, decisions, or behaviors are praiseworthy?
- Share that you appreciate the effort and do not take it for granted. Thank them for bringing that strength to the company.

Conditions for Delivering Corrective Feedback

Given that everyone has an ego and does not like to be criticized, corrective feedback will be received best under a few conditions. There are three questions to ask yourself before delivering any corrective feedback or anything that can be viewed as criticism:

- Are you the right person to give corrective feedback in this situation?
- Have you built a foundation of trust through the first three levels of maturity and positive feedback first?
- Is what you are going to say in their best interest? (Will it help improve performance? Is it given because you care about this person's success, quality of work, or relationships?)

    We will examine each of these questions in the following sections.

Are You the Right Person to Give Corrective Feedback in This Situation?

The negativity bias makes it easy for us to point out faults in someone else, but we do not have the authority to tell someone on the street how to live or how to do their job. People who do this are usually perceived as nosy at best and can easily put themselves in a confrontational situation. As I write this, I remember my younger sister chanting, "You're not the boss of me!" when we were kids. Technically she was right.

> In any situation, corrective feedback should only come from one of these two sources:
>
> - A person in a position of authority
> - Someone in a personal relationship with you who genuinely wants the best for you

People in a position of authority include the following:

- **A manager, team leader, or company owner** has the responsibility and authority of giving feedback that is in their employees' best interests and that helps them succeed in their role because they are responsible for the outcome of work that effects the company's products or services.

- **Customers** have authority to provide feedback as the ultimate end users of your products or services. Most people do so online for everyone to see, and their online reviews drive more purchase decisions than advertising dollars do.

- Whether or not **colleagues** can provide corrective feedback (or any commentary on performance, even positive) to each other is a gray area and can vary from one company culture to another. The key here is the intention with which it is given and the way it is given. For example, if I have a good relationship with a colleague who is having trouble, I might say, "I know you're having trouble with your closing percentage, and I noticed you're not asking a few key questions when you're on the phone with potential clients. I have some suggestions if you want them." Any spirit of competition or condescension must be removed. You must have the recipient's best interest at heart.

- **Experts** like doctors, lawyers, or consultants give feedback as part of why we consulted them in the first place; in other words, we ask (and usually pay) for their opinions and feedback.

- **A parent, teacher, mentor, or other nonbusiness authority in your life** must constantly be giving guidance and corrective feedback in their role to help you become the best person you can be.

In a personal peer relationship, neither person has authority over another; therefore the question of whether to give corrective feedback to someone must come from the intention behind it. If you are trying to criticize, to hurt them, to compete with them, or to point out faults, then your intentions will come through louder than your specific comments. Even if you want the best for someone and you have good intentions to try and help them, your words may be met with resistance because all criticism is difficult for us to hear.

In personal relationships, giving unsolicited feedback should be reserved for times you observe self-destructive behavior or something on which you can provide help or advice because you care about this person and want them to be happy and successful in life. In that case you should bear in mind that you may be risking the relationship by delivering feedback where it wasn't requested, and where you may not have the "authority" to do so. You should only do it to save them from the negative consequences of their behavior that you observe or foresee. Relationship feedback is almost always going to be based on opinion, which means the recipient might be offended, call you judgmental, tell you to mind your own business, or walk away from the friendship. In a peer relationship it is wise to give negative feedback only for jugular or self-destructive issues.

Have You Built a Foundation of Trust through Positive Feedback First?

Before you can give corrective feedback, you have to build a foundation of trust through positive feedback. This is critical to developing the skill of providing effective feedback that can raise someone else's performance level or have a positive impact on their relationships.

Everyone wants to hear that they're doing something right. Responding to positive reinforcement is an instinct we're born with. Parents must constantly reinforce positive behavior that they want to be repeated by their children and correct the behaviors that they do not want repeated. Kids need an immense amount of correction over the course of growing up, so if we never take the time to praise or compliment their work ethic, their accomplishments, their efforts, their kindness, their good behaviors, and their good decisions, then the bulk of our interaction with them over time will be corrective feedback or criticism. Any parent of a teenager can tell you how well that will be received. If I consistently give positive feedback and praise when it is deserved, then when the situation arises that requires corrective feedback, it will be easier to give, and easier for them to receive.

The same is true for adults – we want to hear when we're doing something right. Giving someone positive feedback builds trust by demonstrating that you're working in their best interest, gives them the acknowledgment they need and deserve, and encourages positive behaviors, habits, decisions, or efforts to be repeated. If this has been established, then when corrective feedback is necessary it can be quick, concise, direct, and honest, and it can be trusted.

Is What You Are Going to Say in Their Best Interest?

The ultimate litmus test for whether to give corrective feedback is the intention behind it. Are you trying to help this person, or harm them? There is a fine line between corrective feedback, often called *constructive criticism*, and insult. If your ego is threatened and you have put yourself in competition with someone, you will find fault with whatever they're doing, how they work, how they look, or how they breathe. Your criticism will not come from a desire to help them succeed because it is not actually intended to help them; it's intended to help you feel better about yourself by criticizing them. That intent will be evident to the recipient and will not be effective, even if it addresses a real problem they have.

Before giving corrective feedback, prepare by asking yourself a few questions:

- Is it necessary?
- Will it help them improve their performance or the quality of their work or relationships?
- Are you giving it because you care about this person?
- Do you have a solution or helpful advice to offer, instead of just pointing out a weakness?

If you can answer yes to any of these questions, then your corrective feedback has the potential to help the recipient improve their work or relationship experience.

For example, at one of my first jobs I had a friend who used to complain and joke about his wife while we were in settings like group lunches or team meetings. It made people uncomfortable, and it made him untrustworthy and unlikeable to some people in the office. I was too young to know what to do at the time, but if that happened today, I would speak to him privately and maybe suggest reflecting on some difficult questions like: What is really going on here? Do you need marriage counseling? Are you being too demanding? Do you need more communication with your wife? Are you divulging too much personal information at work? Are you doing this because you have a problem you do not know how to solve?

Without asking for answers to personal matters, I would offer to talk if he wanted to, and I would suggest that he should be less critical of his wife in public out of respect for their relationship privacy, to stop making people feel uncomfortable in the office, and to stop sabotaging his own professional reputation by doing what he was doing. By addressing his tendency to complain about his wife without his request for my opinion, I would be jeopardizing our colleague relationship. If he decided that I overstepped, and my opinion was not welcome even though I had his best interest in mind, then I would ask him to at least not do it in front of me anymore. I would have no control over his decision to end our relationship, and so I would only address his behavior over a jugular issue like this one that I thought was self-destructive and worrisome, and where I thought I could provide some help if he were willing to accept it.

The Corrective Feedback Script

My father-in-law ran a small business with a busy warehouse for decades, and many young people came to work there over the years. When he had to fire someone, he would say, "Go see

Jackie," and leave the room. The oblivious worker would go find my mother-in-law in the office and say, "Dave told me to come see you . . . ?" Then she had to say, "That means you're fired; here's your check. Sorry." He did not have the heart to fire a worker even if they could not handle the job. "Go see Jackie" has become folklore-status lingo in our family for "you screwed up."

I have a tech industry client whose board of directors approved and went through with a global reorganization with the hidden agenda of getting rid of three of the company's seven executives. All this because no one on the board knew how to get rid of those three who were not performing.

This is a very common problem. Most people do not like to deliver bad news, so they avoid giving corrective feedback, then poor habits continue, and eventually the employee could make a mistake so egregious that they expose themselves to being fired.

You cannot become an expert at something without some failures and course correction along the way, so corrective feedback is a necessary part of the learning process in a career, sport, or any endeavor. Recognizing positive behaviors and correcting negative behaviors is the way to help someone learn and improve. The key is to deliver corrective feedback in a way that has the best chance of changing the behavior because the goal of feedback is improvement. You do not want poor delivery to get in the way of that.

Delivering feedback effectively is the most valuable leadership skill in the corporate world.

The negativity bias makes us ultra-sensitive to criticism, so if you have built trust with this person by giving positive feedback when it is due, then when there is corrective feedback to give, just make it quick. That's all that's needed. Your words will be heard. Just like with the Broken Agreement Script, this should be done privately without an audience where someone else can hear what is being said, to avoid a poor outcome that results simply because of the environment in which the feedback was delivered, and then no improvement will happen.

Here are some examples:

- "Joe, you haven't been using the correct subject line on your campaign emails. This is how I want them to go out. Use this one from now on, okay?"

- "Alyssa, you're scheduling your calls too close together and you're rushing off the phone with clients. Leave a buffer of ten minutes in between each one so you don't sound rushed, okay?"

- "Marc, I can hear your conversations from across the room. You have to be a little quieter at your desk, okay?"

- "Angela, when you walk in at 8:00 a.m., it means a customer could be waiting at the door for you to arrive and open the doors. You have to be here by 7:50 a.m., okay?"

- "Ray, your numbers are low so far this month. Let me know if you want to go over a plan to get them up by the end of the month so you can make quota, okay?"

Each of these critiques would take less than eight seconds to say to these employees. As their manager, I am the right person to deliver this feedback. I have already built a culture of trust with them because I pay attention to their performance and I freely give positive reinforcement wherever it is deserved. What I have to say is in their best interest because it is intended to help them improve future results from their performance. I have chosen the right environment where no one else can hear the feedback. All the conditions are met for me to give this feedback. All I have to do is say what I have to say directly, clearly, and quickly. I have confidence that they will hear my words and act on this feedback. When I say "okay?" at the end of the feedback, I am asking for their verbal agreement to act on it. If they agree to act on my feedback but do not follow through, or they fail to rectify the issue I have addressed, then I can use the Broken Agreement Script (see Chapter 5) to address that issue further.

The Corrective Feedback Script

If the subject matter of the feedback that's necessary is personal or sensitive, then you will need this script:

1. State that you have an insight or observation to share that is intended to help them and ask for their permission to provide feedback.

   "I have an observation that I think will help you moving forward. I only share this with you because I want you to be successful. Are you open to hearing it?"

2. Share the feedback directly and concisely. Do not exaggerate data by using absolutes. This is a trick of the ego to reinforce your point. Remove the ego from the conversation. Absolutes like always, never, all the time, and every day are rarely 100% true and will open the door to refute your feedback as untrue. Instead preface it with "There are times when . . ." and then share the feedback. It will sound like this:

   "There are times when . . ."

   ". . . you cut people off when they are talking."

   ". . . you do not speak up when you could help the team."

". . . you shut down if your opinion does not win."

". . . you engage in side-conversations during meetings and it's distracting."

". . . you give people the silent treatment when you get upset."

3. Ask for their thoughts or whether they have noticed this behavior, if appropriate, or simply wait for them to respond.

   "What are your thoughts?"

   "What do you think?"

   "Do you notice this?"

4. Gain agreement that the behavior will change in the future. Agree on new behaviors and desired impact. If appropriate to the behavior in question, suggest an incremental follow-up to check on progress with the new behavior:

   "I would like to see you be more vocally supportive in our meetings. I think this will help you be viewed more benevolently by your colleagues."

5. Share your intent again if they are defensive or if you think this feedback was particularly difficult to hear. Thank them for having an uncomfortable conversation.

   "Again, I only shared this with you because I want you to be successful. Thank you for being open to having this conversation."

6. Give positive feedback and praise when you see that performance is improved and at incremental follow-ups, if any.

   "I noticed that you complimented Vince's idea in the meeting. Thank you for your commitment to the team. I think your colleagues responded well to it. Great job!"

Corrective Feedback Script Example #1

Here is an example of a client who used the full script to address his employee's weakness, which was failure to take charge of her project meetings.

Max:	Melissa, I have an observation to share that I hope will help you in your client meetings. Are you open to hearing it?
Melissa:	Yes, what is it?
Max:	There are times when you do not take control of your meetings and they just wander, leaving your team and your client feeling uncertain of your ability to handle the account. This can lead to us losing this client if they feel their time or money is being wasted, as well as your team members and subsequently the leadership of our company losing confidence in you. Do you notice this happening?
Melissa:	I have noticed, but I don't know exactly what to do differently.
Max:	I have suggestions for you, and I'm willing to coach you. Will you agree to that?
Melissa:	Yes, that would be helpful.
Max:	Great, let's set up a weekly session the day before your client meetings for two or three weeks and see how it goes. Thanks, Melissa!

My client, Max, thought the employee would benefit from follow-up coaching based on the corrective feedback he provided. He coached her on developing and sticking to meeting agendas, more directly communicating with team members and subcontractors, and regular check-ins with the client to help improve her meeting performance. After several coaching sessions Melissa's team members reported that she performed much better, and her client seemed much more confident with the progress of the project.

Corrective Feedback Script Example #2

Another client, Janet, was new in her management role, and she had started regularly giving positive feedback to her employees, but she struggled with delivering feedback that people did not want to hear. She had an employee whose talent was an asset to the company, but who had a weakness that was threatening his career and relationships at work. She used the Corrective Feedback Script to bring this to his attention, but she felt that it did not require regular follow-ups to check on progress; she believed a one-time discussion was more appropriate.

Janet: Andrew, I have an insight that I think might help you, and I only share this with you because I want you to be more successful in our group meetings. Would you be open to hearing it?

Andrew: Okay, shoot.

Janet: There are times when you cut people off or talk over people when they are talking, including customers. This is frustrating for the person speaking and for the others who are listening. I do not want to see this get in the way of a sale or of you being successful in your relationships. Are you aware that you're doing that?

Andrew: No, I wasn't aware.

Janet: I think if you wait for a pause to make sure they're finished speaking it will improve your colleague and customer relationships. Can you watch out for that next time?

Andrew: Got it.

Janet: Okay, thanks for listening.

If this issue comes up again with Andrew, it will be easier for Janet to address it as a broken agreement. By sharing her intent and keeping it short and direct, she was able to approach Andrew with a spirit of wanting to help him. By learning how to deliver feedback effectively, she was able to start mentoring her employees, concentrate on their strengths, and work around their weaknesses.

Corrective Feedback Script Example #3

This script saved someone's job a long time ago. Jim was a guy in the office who had poor hygiene habits. To put it bluntly, he smelled bad. People began protesting being on his project teams because they had to work in close quarters with him. Of course, no one said anything directly to Jim. It was office gossip at its worst. I heard the rumor that the manager had decided to fire him. Jim had gone out of his way to offer expertise on something for me in the past, and I felt loyalty to him, so I not only wanted to help him, but I also saw the value that his expertise brought to me and the other salespeople in the company, and I knew that losing him would be detrimental to our company. I asked the manager to hold off so I could talk to Jim privately first. Since this is a sensitive issue, I used a modified version of the Corrective Feedback Script so that I could keep it as brief as possible. The conversation went like this:

Steve: Jim, can I talk to you about something personal?

Jim
(curious): Yes.

Steve: I only share this with you because I want you to be successful. There are times when your body odor gets in the way of your work. Your career opportunities may be suffering because of it, and I do not want to see that. Think about it, okay? Thanks for letting me be candid with you.

I did not put him on the spot to answer. I just walked away when he nodded. Jim did improve his hygiene habits, and we never mentioned it again. The intent was crucial to it being received well. Both Jim and I handled the situation with Level Four Maturity. I did not deliver any insults or low blows; he did not protest and attack me or the news I was giving him. It must have been hard for him to hear, but it was given in a spirit of wanting to help him be successful, and he was mature enough to handle it. Jim and I were equal colleagues, so I did not have a position of authority in our relationship. I was coming to him as someone who cared about his success, but by offering corrective feedback I risked offending him and ending our relationship. It was worth it because I did not want him to get fired. If it was given in a spirit of criticism, then it might not have been received well by him, and he probably would have wound up quitting or being fired.

Corrective Feedback Script Example #4

I had a client getting many complaints about Mac, a district manager. Turnover was high on Mac's team. He was edgy to say the least, and he called himself a "self-proclaimed jerk." Mac's perspective was that he was very good at his technical position; he knew how to do the job so everyone should listen to him and put up with his personality. Yes, this guy really said that.

The executive team that made a significant initial investment in hiring Mac decided to fire him rather than let the rest of the district continue to crumble under him. Because of his abrupt and confrontational style, they did not trust him to go quietly after being fired for cause, and so they wanted to go above and beyond and cover their bases under employment law. That's when they asked me to deliver a Leading Relationships workshop, so that they could check the box of trying to assimilate him into the company culture before they fired him. I agreed to do it, and also suggested to the executive team that I coach *them* on delivering effective feedback as well.

In my opinion they needed a combination of the Broken Agreement Script, to hold him accountable for the company values of respect and treating others the way you want to be treated, which Mac was not honoring, and the Corrective Feedback Script, to coach him along the way. They needed to establish that Mac's behavior was now in the way of his paycheck. If Mac was not open to receiving training, coaching, or feedback and aligning his style with company values, then he would either be selecting himself out of the company without being fired, or they would be establishing cause to fire him without repercussions. It turned out that Mac did not even show up for the company workshop, which led the company leadership to assume that he knew it was about him. This is an example of how you cannot coach everyone out of their own way. The company fired him, but they also accepted my suggestion of coaching the leaders on giving effective feedback, addressing broken agreements, and smart hiring criteria.

If you establish a culture of continuous improvement through effective delivery of positive and corrective feedback, then feedback becomes easier to give and easier to receive for everyone.

Feedback in Personal Relationships

This script is also a valuable communication tool for personal relationships because no relationship is perfect. Positive feedback in personal relationships comes in the form of compliments, recognition of gestures, expressing appreciation of someone's place in your life or the way they treat you, and telling someone what you like about them and about your relationship. Or even more subtle expressions of appreciation like being the one to reach out to plan something together, texting, calling, sending jokes, or any level of engagement in the friendship. We have all had one-sided relationships where this type of engagement is absent, and you know the other person does not appreciate you or the relationship the way you do. Even my brother – the lowest-maintenance person I know – stopped asking me to get together after I had turned him down due to other obligations three or four times in a row this year. Of course, he added expletives and told me he's not calling me until I call him first because that's what brothers do. He felt one-sidedness in the relationship, which was totally fair, and I had to make it up to him because I want to continue a good relationship with him.

Every relationship, whether it is considered high or low maintenance, has an acceptable level of engagement, feedback, and a style of expression for appreciation of the other person. If you care enough about the other person and the relationship to give both positive and corrective feedback when it is needed, in whatever style the relationship has established, the relationship can thrive and avoid problems that come from withholding feelings and letting the ego take over.

Receiving Feedback Graciously

Both the person giving and the person receiving the feedback must approach the situation with Level Four Maturity for it to be successful and produce good results that improve performance and strengthen communication. If one of them lets their ego get in the way of the message, then only negative results can be produced. If we do not know where we need improvement then we cannot fix the problem, and so receiving feedback maturely and implementing it despite feeling vulnerable is a necessary skill for continuous improvement.

How have you responded to corrective feedback in the past? Do you get defensive? Do you launch counterattacks, pointing out the other person's weaknesses in return? Do you shut down and give the silent treatment? Do you get wounded and punish the messenger by passive-aggressively making something difficult for them?

Although a response like that is a failure at Level Four Maturity, it is instinctive, and many people do react that way. Our instinct is to defend ourselves because when we hear anything that can be taken as criticism, the ego is threatened and defenses are heightened. Some people are just not mature enough to overcome this because their ego is in the way, even if the feedback is given by someone who wants the best for them, and they recognize that the feedback given is valid. It would be in their best interest to improve and rid themselves of this weakness or problem, but instead they try to justify every mistake and then blame others for anything imperfect in the relationship.

This is typical of someone whose goal is perfection rather than continuous improvement. The ego is the biggest obstacle they will face in improving their skills, relationships, and talents. Instead of wanting to improve, they want to be told they are already perfect, and they perceive corrective feedback as unfair criticism or hostility instead of an opportunity to grow and improve.

If your goal is to continuously get better, then corrective feedback is the fastest path to pursue that, so when someone presents you with an "opportunity for improvement," take it.

Corrective feedback from a trusted manager who wants to help you improve is your most helpful asset on the path to continuous improvement. Any time an opportunity to improve presents itself, your unbiased reaction should be gratitude that someone noticed and cared enough to offer you advice on how to get better at something. This is going to be much easier if the feedback is given respectfully, by someone who has the authority to give it, and it is meant for your best interest. But you cannot control how it is given, only how you receive it and, if it's true, use it as an opportunity to improve. Control your ego and listen to the message. You cannot pursue continuous improvement without being able to receive feedback with Level Four Maturity.

The true test of Level Four Maturity is accepting corrective feedback even if your ego is hurt. Some appropriate Level Four responses to corrective feedback are:

- "Thank you for caring enough to want the best for me."
- "I can't get better unless I get feedback, so thank you."
- "I appreciate your perspective. I will consider it."
- "Can you clarify for me so I know what specifically to do differently?"
- "Can you give me some advice on how to improve?"
- "I am committed to improving, and I know this feedback will help me do that."

Level Four is the plateau of most relationships. Very few of our interactions with co-workers, roommates, family, friends, or neighbors on a daily basis will get to Level Five interactions. If we can be vulnerable and care for the vulnerability of others enough to admit our mistakes, apologize when necessary, accept others' apologies when they admit mistakes, provide feedback that raises the performance of others, give and receive feedback graciously, concentrate on each other's strengths, and work around each other's weaknesses, then we can lead these relationships to be successful, healthy, and fulfilling. We can derive joy from our relationships and avoid the biggest contributor to stress, which is dysfunctional relationships.

Level Four Quick Reference Guide

Success at Level Four Maturity is admitting mistakes, apologizing when necessary, concentrating on each other's strengths, working around each other's weaknesses, providing positive and corrective feedback in a way that improves performance and cares for the vulnerability of others, and receiving feedback graciously.

Failure at Level Four Maturity includes denying or blaming someone else for our own weaknesses or mistakes, not apologizing when we should, exposing or attacking someone else's weaknesses for our own benefit, withholding positive feedback, and bolstering one's own ego by criticizing someone's mistakes or weaknesses.

How to proceed with the relationship if someone fails at Level Four Maturity: If someone fails at Level Four interactions, revert to only Level One, Two, or Three interactions if possible. If the relationship must continue in a team setting, use the Corrective Feedback Script to address a weakness that cannot be worked around.

Skills learned: Learn the ingredients to a good apology. Concentrate on strengths, work around weaknesses. Separate positive and negative feedback. Use the Corrective Feedback Script for sensitive or personal issues.

8

Level Five: Understanding Intrinsic and Extrinsic Motivators

How many people know what job you have, how long you have worked there, and the name of your boss? How many people know where you live? These facts are easy to obtain, and we are rarely guarded about sharing the basic facts of our employment and the town we live in. We hand out business cards with contact information, we have small talk with strangers, we want people to be able to find us online, we make connections all the time. But if you ask some next-level questions, you may not get candid, complete, honest answers so quickly.

- Why did you take the job you currently have?
- Why did you accept the salary level you are currently at instead of a higher-paying job?
- Why did you choose to live where you live?
- What motivates you to get out of bed each day and go to work?
- What do you want out of your career?
- Where do you want to be in a few years? How long do you want to stay where you are?
- What do you want to change or improve about your career and your life?
- What are your priorities, and how have they changed over the years?
- Who and what is most important to you?
- What are you willing to accept or sacrifice in order to provide for or protect those people, places, or causes that are most important to you?

Success at Level Five Maturity is understanding someone's intrinsic and extrinsic motivators and working in their best interest to help them meet those needs.

Whys and Wants

The whys and wants of our choices can be highly personal. They can be tied to our most vital relationships, our most vital beliefs, our most vital connections to people or ideas or places, our background, our comfort zone, and our goals. Even if someone told you all about their family, their hometown, and their career goals, they may not share everything with you. There might be a fragile relationship that is keeping them in a certain city, or a personal experience that makes who they work for much more important to them than salary, or a specific benefit like a medical coverage, a tuition reimbursement, or a vacation package that is more important than salary because of a variety of reasons that they may not want to share.

Refer to the Employee Motivation Checklist (see Figure 3.1 in Chapter 3). It lists many reasons why you might work where you work and asks you to rank them in order of importance to you in your current position. Would you rank fair and respectful treatment at work as more important than annual salary increases? Would you rank contributing to the greater good as more important than living in your first-choice city? Deciding to accept a job offer is a delicate balance and a total package compromise of many different life factors because it has to check many boxes for you so you can thrive in that position and be satisfied for an acceptable period of time.

These whys and wants that we work to satisfy are our intrinsic motivators. Intrinsic motivators are the things we do for pure enjoyment or personal satisfaction, for love, passion, curiosity, fun, purpose, meaning, or growth. You don't need me to motivate you to seek them. You will work and sacrifice for these things. If I know what your whys and wants and needs are, I can either help you achieve them, or I can use them against you when it benefits me. Extrinsic motivators are everything we do to avoid consequences. Some things can be both intrinsic and extrinsic motivators. Pursuing a raise or a promotion can be both intrinsic, if you are passionate about your job, and extrinsic, because we need money to live and pay our bills.

Similar to Level Four, letting someone else know the needs we are trying to fulfill and the whys and wants behind our decisions makes us vulnerable. Once someone knows how to push our buttons, if their ego gets involved and they want to play win-lose games with us, they have all the ammunition they need to hurt us in order to win, to make themselves look good, to make sure we lose something important to us, to force us to make a difficult choice, or to gain power or influence over us. Their main goal may not be to hurt us deliberately; they may just have goals that conflict or compete with ours, and if they know what is most important to us it will be easier for them to negotiate a win.

This is a lesson that has roots as early as the first time in my career that I was employed with a large company. A round of layoffs was coming up and the company was trying to save money wherever possible. Unbeknownst to the frontline workers, mid-level management was executing a strategy that entailed creating difficult scenarios for employees in order to manipulate them into quitting, rather than being laid off and thus eligible for separation benefits.

They especially targeted veteran sales reps who were being paid more than the newer reps for doing the same job. The result was that the woman who had the Boston sales territory was transferred to the northwest United States. She quit rather than taking that transfer and moving her family away from their hometown. A man who had had a mustache for 20 years was told to shave it if he wanted a promotion. Having waited for several years for a promotion, to the company's surprise he did it! But he then became so uncomfortable with the way he was treated that he quit. A man who had just had his third child was transferred to a position in which he would have to travel overnight three times a week, putting a significant strain on his family. He quit as well. General treatment of employees by management became harsh and disrespectful, and several people quit because of that.

Many of these stories kept popping up. About a year after the layoffs, I was promoted into a management role, and I was informally trained on this strategy, which they called "coaching people out of the company." The idea was to identify people or roles they wanted to eliminate from the company, or territories they needed to thin out, and find out what would make people quit, then do exactly that so they would leave without the company being legally responsible for layoff benefits or severance packages. This strategy was explained by straight-faced people who did not admit that it was manipulation and exploitation of people's circumstances and lives. Of course, I remembered how it was executed the previous year. My boss had called each person into a one-on-one meeting to "get to know us better" and help "plan our career tracks." The strategy was to find a soft spot, a critical issue that was so important to the employee that they would not compromise on it, and then to attack there.

I've seen this play out in other companies as well. When it was decided that someone should go, the management treated them with general disrespect and withheld common courtesy and kindness as a first line of attack to encourage them to leave, and the employee would think it was their own idea. I did not stay at that company for long after that. Perhaps they used this as a strategy to get rid of me by knowing that I would not participate in it. Not surprisingly, that company went out of business a short time later.

This is an unfortunate but common strategy. The management of the company is trying to win by saving money on salaries and benefits and is using the needs of the employees against them. They have conflicting needs. The manager is trying to get rid of the expense associated with carrying that employee, and the employee has many needs that the manager can refuse to meet so that the employee will leave.

Perhaps the goal is not to make an employee leave but rather to make them work more or do something they would not otherwise have done. I have seen an employee's simple need for a paycheck exploited to the point where they will work harder and longer than is fair, do parts of other people's jobs, and do things that are far outside their job description. I have also seen a manager purposely keep an employee from getting something they wanted because the manager felt threatened by that employee, and even simply because the manager had the power to control whether that employee got what they wanted. It's a case of "I don't get what I want out of life so nobody else should either." Since the manager is in a position of power, the manager is going to win.

This is the classic story of manipulation: now that I know what you want, I can use it against you either to prevent you from getting it, or to get what I want – either way I win. This is the same reason we don't show our cards during a card game. If I know you need a nine, I'm not going to lay down my nine even if I don't need it, until I have what I need to win. That's how games work; someone is always trying to win. It's a classic negotiation tactic as well. If I know what is most important to you, I can probably use that as an incentive to make you bend on other points.

This can be a huge problem in personal relationships as well as business. Have you ever found out that someone you trusted was using your need for friendship or companionship, or taking advantage of your kindness, in order to get what they want or to build themselves up and feel powerful? It's a horrible feeling to be used by someone else for their own gain, and it's even worse if they have exploited a need you had in the process. We open ourselves up to that kind of vulnerability by letting the wrong people know our most important needs.

My client Dom was on a long drive with a co-worker to visit a jobsite, and they talked for a few hours in the car. Dom told his co-worker that one day he would like to open his own business. A few months later they both interviewed for an executive position at the company. The co-worker told the interviewer that Dom's goal was to start his own company so if Dom was hired, they would soon lose him when he decided to start a competing company, but his own goal was to stay there for the duration of his career, so he should get the promotion instead. The co-worker was promoted. Dom asked the CEO what the determining factor was, and he told Dom what the co-worker said. This became an awkward situation, and Dom left the company, but he wasn't ready to start his own company yet, so he had to find another job.

These examples are failures at Level Five Maturity. It's a hard lesson that not everyone works in your best interest. There were probably some clues along the way that should have told you this was coming. In your observation, did this person have failures at Levels One through Four? Did they pretend not to know someone in order to feel more powerful than they are? Did they refuse to speak to someone with whom they had a disagreement? Did they argue facts or change the context of conversations in order to be right? Did they break agreements or not do what they said they would do? Did they disrespect someone else's opinion? Did they refuse to admit it when they made a mistake? Did they pretend to know everything about everything in order to look knowledgeable and feel powerful? If the answers to any of these questions are yes, then they were giving you clues that this might happen someday because someone can't succeed at Level Five Maturity if they can't succeed at Levels One through Four. Before you have a Level Five conversation with someone, you need to see that they have demonstrated success at Levels One through Four.

If someone is capable of success all the way through Level Four, then they are most likely also capable of success at Level Five. Failures at this level most often happen when you have ignored the clues along the way and trusted someone erroneously at Level Five, or you have misjudged their desire for a Level Five relationship. Level Five depends on desire from both people, which is why failures at this level are usually more impactful than failures at lower levels. After reading these examples you can probably see how Level Five failures have toppled leadership, and led to lawsuits, corporate sabotage, personal betrayal, and divorce or long-term relationship damage.

Level Five Comes with High Stakes

The reason we keep trying at Level Five when a failure could be so costly is because success at Level Five can be so beneficial. The risk and reward even out.

Many years ago, I was a sales rep, and I had a boss I trusted. We worked closely together for several years. I told him I eventually wanted to be in the public speaking industry. He found a way to use that intrinsic motivator to help me perform at a higher level in my current role in the company. He partnered me with the public relations department so that I could make media appearances for the company. I didn't even know this opportunity existed, but I was able to do my sales job and also do the media appearances when they came up. If he hadn't demonstrated maturity in all other transactions and relationships that I had observed, I probably would not have trusted him with my goal. He could have used it to weed me out of the company, he could have been jealous and withheld the information about the media opportunities from me just so that I couldn't have that chance to work toward my goal, he could have told others and mocked me for it. Instead, he learned what would really motivate me and used it in my best interest.

That is success at Level Five Maturity. What benefits did he and the company receive because he did this for me? I stayed late. I worked hard. I did whatever he needed whenever he needed it. I stayed longer in that position than I would have otherwise. How smart for our relationship and the company! Because he met my needs, I went out of my way to meet his, I knew he was evaluated on the department's numbers so I did everything I could to support that; I did everything within my control to help him be successful in his role since he was helping me to reach my goal.

When Level Five Is Nonnegotiable

There are a few vital relationships that need to be at Level Five to be functional. The first one we all experience is with our parents. I believe that Level Five Maturity is not on the "nice to have" list of a parent's job description, but rather it is imperative. If a parent doesn't work in the best interest of the child regarding their needs, then they are failing at parenting, and repercussions of this can last a lifetime. Supporting basic survival needs and basic mental, physical, and emotional health needs, as well as encouraging the goals and dreams of a child are all part of a parent's job. Supporting needs is also imperative to spousal relationships. These vital relationships cannot be healthy and functional if one person is always trying to win and using the other's needs against them or taking advantage of the other person's needs to get what they want. Strong friendships also require that we know our friend will not use our most personal intrinsic motivators against us. These close family and friend relationships involve sharing needs with each other and helping each other meet those needs. It would be great to know that you can trust your family and friends at Level Five.

Good leadership requires this level of trustworthiness as well. What is the confidence level that people have in you? If an employee, colleague, or friend shares a need or a dream they have with you, can they be confident that you won't talk behind their back, or use it against them to build your own self-image, achieve your own agenda, or sacrifice their needs in order to meet your own? Can they be confident that you will only use that information to help them achieve their dream or meet their need, or encourage them as they seek to do that?

At the highest level of maturity in relationships, people trust that you won't sacrifice their needs in order to meet your own. This means putting other people's needs before our own. Remember that relationships don't work if competition gets involved and someone is trying to win. They only work when two people get their needs met. I meet your needs, and you meet mine, or else our relationship will suffer or fail. As an employer, if you cannot meet my needs for growth and development, for respect and recognition, and for fair compensation, then it is not a good fit for me anymore. The relationship will fail, and I will look for work elsewhere. That means your need for an employee is unfulfilled. Therefore, meeting my needs is the only way to get your own needs met in the relationship.

Understanding this and supporting the needs of the people in our lives is success at Level Five Maturity. Relationships between two people who can be successful at Level Five Maturity are personally the most satisfying relationships we experience, and in business they are the most productive and profitable. Our most trusted relationships require Level Five Maturity.

Level Five Quick Reference Guide

Success at Level Five Maturity is understanding someone's intrinsic and extrinsic motivators and working in their best interest to help them meet those needs.

Failure at Level Five Maturity is using someone's driving needs or private information against them to manipulate, control, or exploit them, or "push their buttons."

How to proceed with the relationship if someone fails at Level Five Maturity: If someone fails at Level Five interactions, the stakes are higher than at the other levels. You probably will not be able to just revert to friendly and supportive Level Four interactions after that. There can be hurt or betrayed feelings that can make that impossible. If this is a significant relationship in your life that needs to function well at Level Five, you can use the Broken Agreement Script from Level Two to address the failure. If the person gives a sincere apology, including a commitment that the failure won't happen again, then you can move forward if you both wish to do so. Most times after a failure at Level Five, someone will wind up leaving the company because it will be too difficult to work together anymore. Partnerships can dissolve, and even marriages and friendships can break up. If it is possible to revert to lower-level interactions, then do that. But if not, you may need to start a future without that person.

Skills learned: Appreciate the people in your life who can succeed at Level Five Maturity. Always care for the needs and motivators of others and seek to use them in the best interest of that person.

3

Use the Five Levels of Maturity as a Leadership Handbook

As you are out there thriving at Level Five, you may observe other people's behavior and discover that they are not interacting as maturely as they could be with each other. This can make you realize that you are far ahead of these people on a relationship scale, and that can easily turn relationship maturity into a competition, leading you to feel superior to them. This is a trap of your ego, which can lead you to regress and fail at all of the levels. This is where *leading the relationship* comes in. You have an opportunity to lead people to a higher level of maturity by your example. Whether they follow your lead is up to their ego, as well as to their desire and ability to grow. Set the tone for how you want the relationship to proceed by concentrating on their strengths, managing their weaknesses, treating them how you would want to be treated, and leading the relationship by your example.

With the knowledge and ability to lead your relationships you can subdue the competition and games that plague organizations so that you can radically improve engagement among your team members, focus on your customer, and drive your business forward.

Part 3 explains the benefits that come with Level Five Leadership, along with the most impactful way to use the Five Levels of Maturity in your business.

CHAPTER

9

Managing the Maturity Level of Others

There are many reasons why someone might get stuck at a particular level, and they can be as varied as the backgrounds and experiences people bring to their relationships. I knew a guy in high school who would walk by people in the halls holding his head straight and high. He wouldn't acknowledge people and would pretend not to know people's names. He may have wanted people to think he was tougher or more popular than they were, and many described him as unfriendly or conceited. He consistently failed at Level One basic maturity. The thing is, I had known him in middle school too, and I was there when his friends humiliated him in front of a crowd of people once. Of course, they thought it was funny, but he didn't, and I knew what it did to him. Watching him in high school, it made sense that he had decided he would never be rejected or humiliated by anyone ever again. I don't know him as an adult. It's possible that he has forgiven those guys and has moved beyond what happened to him years ago and he has healthy, respectful relationships with people today. It is also possible that he has not moved on, and to this day he still gets his self-image from making sure that he is the one to ignore or put others down before they can do it to him.

I know a woman who suffered ostracizing as a child. Even many years later she tends to be guarded with people and assume they don't really like her. She assumes that people will take advantage of her if they get the chance. She doesn't trust anyone to act at Level Five Maturity with her.

After one of my presentations a man approached me and said:

"I just realized that I have a problem. I never apologize. I was in a car accident when I was 16 years old, and I was shaken up, and I apologized to the other driver. The insurance company, my parents, and our lawyer said because I apologized, the other side was able to

*contend that the accident was my fault, and my parents were sued
for a lot of money. They told me never to apologize. I was so affected
by that, and I just realized that I have applied it to all situations.
I never admit when I'm wrong, and I have been damaging my relationships for 10 years. I was stuck and couldn't move to Level Four
because of it."*

Everyone brings their life experiences with them to relationships because those experiences contribute to our character development, how well we communicate, how we perceive others, how
quickly we trust, and how we react to disappointments. It would
be easy if you could just ask someone when you first meet them
what their level of maturity in relationships is, but most people
are not aware of what they are not capable of in relationships,
of what holds them back, and of where their failures are, and so
most people would assume that they themselves are capable of
the highest level of maturity. They get caught up in the details of
each individual situation and how someone else is always wrong,
and they don't recognize patterns of behavior, especially their
own. Being aware of the level of maturity at which the people
around you can be successful with others helps you know what
you can expect from them and therefore helps prevent problems
in the relationship.

What Are Your Relationship Biases?

There is an old parable of travelers that illustrates this:

*Back in the days when the settlers were moving to the West, a wise man
stood on a hill outside a new Western town. As the settlers came from
the East, the wise man was the first person they met before coming to
the settlement. They asked eagerly what the people of the town were like.*

*He answered them with a question: "What were the people like in the
town you just left?"*

Some said, "The town we came from was wicked. The people were rude gossips who took advantage of innocent people. It was filled with thieves and liars."

The wise man answered, "This town is the same as the one you left."

They thanked the man for saving them from the trouble they had just come out of. They then moved on further west.

Then another group of settlers arrived and asked the same question: "What is this town like?"

The wise man asked again, "What was the town like where you came from?" These responded, "It was wonderful! We had dear friends. Everyone looked out for the others' interest. There was never any lack because all cared for one another. If someone had a big project, the entire community gathered to help. It was a hard decision to leave, but we felt compelled to make way for future generations by going west as pioneers."

The wise old man said to them exactly what he had said to the other group: "This town is the same as the one you left."

These people responded with joy, "Let's settle here!"[1]

The wise man knew that how we judge others has much to do with our own perspective and that most people will reciprocate if we treat them well and also reciprocate if we treat them poorly. If we are inclined toward good-natured, mature treatment of others, then we may be able to expect to "raise all boats" and receive similar treatment in return. People who are inclined toward petty, untrusting, selfish, or mean-spirited treatment of others may anticipate that is how others will treat them, and so they exude preemptive rudeness and put up walls to maintain distance and do not develop healthy relationships with those around them. Most of the time you don't know anything about someone's relationship proficiency before you interact with them. If you progress too quickly and go beyond someone's ability to reciprocate, you may wind up being disappointed.

Can You Coach Someone to a Higher Level of Maturity?

If two people in a relationship are at different levels of maturity, then their relationship will eventually function best at the lower of the two levels because one of the two people cannot handle interactions at a higher level. This is not the same as giving up on that person or on the relationship. On the contrary, it is usually in both parties' best interest because failure at a higher level will cause problems, disappointment, hurt feelings, or other conflict.

If you have a mentor relationship with that person, you can offer feedback and coach them to progress through these levels and grow in maturity. The goal should be to help them improve how they communicate and interact with people, which will improve their job performance. Perhaps an even more important byproduct of that will ideally be to help them improve their quality of life by improving how they approach all their relationships.

You must decide if you have the kind of relationship with someone where they will accept your coaching or feedback regarding how maturely they handle relationships. If they are willing to accept that guidance and grow in maturity, then it will certainly be worth your investment in the relationship to help them. Unfortunately, I find that many people who struggle with maturity tend to refuse advice that suggests they should change how they do things. That's part of being immature. It takes Level Four Maturity to admit faults and vulnerabilities, and to accept advice from someone else on how to be a better person or how to fix the problems in one's life that their behavior may have caused. If someone is not successful at Level Four Maturity, then they will not be able to admit that they need coaching on being more mature.

Realistically, in most of your relationships you don't have that kind of authority or influence. If you are not a parent, boss, mentor, or elder authority figure in someone's life, then they probably don't want to take feedback from you. Even in those relationships it is sometimes difficult to offer direction. The key is to figure out where someone is and where we can be successful with them and then to operate at that level.

What to Do If Someone Fails

If someone in your life fails at Level Five, then don't go there with them anymore. Unless this is a vitally important relationship in your life, then it is not necessary to have Level Five conversations with someone if they cannot handle them maturely. In fact, if you push, it may hurt you more than it can help you.

If they fail at Level Four and won't ask for help when they need it or won't admit a mistake or apologize for a wrongdoing, then remind them that everyone has flaws and shortcomings. Make a new agreement with them by saying, "Let's just agree that this will not happen again or that in the future we will work with the values of the company in mind, okay?" Now you know that you cannot expect an apology or admission of mistakes from this person. You will have to adjust how you work with them in the future accordingly.

If they fail at Level Three and they take a "my way or the highway" approach to opinions, then don't share opinions with them anymore; just go back to Level Two. If you must work with them, then build a business case for everything. That creates a common goal of pleasing the customer, and everything you do as a team should be directed at that goal.

If they fail at Level Two by not honoring their agreements, then use the Broken Agreement Script (see Chapter 5). If you can't even share facts with them without their ego getting in the way, then, if possible, simply go back to Level One and say hello and goodbye civilly. It's called Level One because even though some people fail at this basic level, it is a minimum standard of maturity that you should hold *yourself* to, even if the other person fails here. You should always be successful at Level One with everyone. No matter what problems you have had with someone, you should be able to acknowledge them out of basic human respect.

If you find that you can no longer have a relationship with someone and you commit to reverting to Level One interactions, would you discuss it with them? I have asked this question in my workshops, and the most common answer someone will give is they would just stop answering communications and blow the person off until they got the message that the relationship is over, and most people in the room nod their heads in approval of that strategy. Although this strategy is common, relationships don't have to end with storming off, ghosting texts, or hoping they "get the message." You can say, "This is no longer a good fit. We're not meeting each other's needs, but I wish you the best," and part ways peacefully without the dissonance of one person wondering what happened.

You can't change the way someone else handles relationships. You can only focus on your own maturity and the way you treat people regardless of their position in life. You can gain people's confidence, build better relationships, be more effective in business, and grow in maturity by minimizing the voice of the ego when you are interacting with others, and by resisting the urge to define yourself by how you size up against another person.

In the relationships you choose, as with friends, partners, and employees you hire, you can choose people who can interact successfully at Level Five Maturity. In the relationships in your life that you don't choose, as with family members, neighbors, colleagues, bosses, and customers, you can remain capable of acting at Level Five Maturity yourself and interact at each level of maturity that is appropriate for the relationship and that the other person can handle successfully. You can move through the levels with someone in this way. If they are responsive and successful at Level One by always acknowledging you in an acceptable way, then you can assume they are capable of Level Two interactions. If they can handle factual exchanges and basic agreements, then you can assume they are capable of Level Three interactions, and so on. Once a failure at any of the levels happens, then you should take a step back and settle into a relationship with them at their level of proficiency. For example, if conversations between you and a colleague get strained when opinions are expressed, then it is probably best to settle into a Level Two relationship, which can be successful, instead of butting heads on politics, sports, or any other opinion-heavy topic. You can sustain a stress-free working relationship with this person if you stay away from opinions, vulnerabilities, and needs, and stick to acknowledgment, facts, and honoring the business agreements you need to make together. By being aware of the maturity level of those around you, you can manage their weaknesses and have successful relationships with them.

Knowing Which Relationships You Can Take to a Higher Level

Even if I am capable of Level Five in every relationship, it doesn't mean that every relationship will go there. I've been going to the same barber for about a year now. We have light, friendly conversation while he cuts my hair. We may occasionally exchange an opinion on something of minimal importance, but he doesn't share his career or personal relationship needs with me. If he did, I might think it's weird, and I would probably find someone else to cut my hair because my barber and I don't need to have a Level Five relationship.

This can be the case with colleagues, neighbors, acquaintances, friends-of-friends, customers, and school parents. Some people want to keep others at a distance for their own reasons, even if they are capable of Level Five relationships. This can usually be accomplished while maintaining simple respect and kindness.

Years ago, I lived in a semi-urban neighborhood where the houses were very close together. I had a neighbor who wanted to maintain clearly defined privacy boundaries. He would give a simple wave occasionally, and when we came face to face, he would say hello with a smile and a nod, and he would respond if someone said, "Isn't this a beautiful day?" but it was clear he didn't want a friendship with someone living so close to him. He didn't want to be put on the spot to have small talk outside regularly, he didn't want to have a borrow-lend relationship, and he didn't want anything more than "I'll call 911 if your house is on fire." He was a guy with a friendly and kind wife, kids who (I assume) love him, a job, and friends and family who visited often. He seems like a guy who is capable of a Level Five relationship when he wants one. He never went below Level One with me or the other neighbors. He would always greet people in a consistent and acceptable way, and once I ran into him in a store and we both smiled and said hi. I had no complaints about this guy at all. I didn't try to go to Level Two or Three and get burned and then settle in at Level One with him. I didn't find that he wasn't capable of a deeper relationship. He just didn't want one, and he made that known to everyone from the day he moved in. He and I were two Level Five people who maintained a Level One relationship because we didn't fit into each other's lives in any way that was more significant than that. That is a successful relationship. I could even argue that we had an unspoken agreement to remain strictly cordial, which would be success at Level Two, and that I honored his opinion or preference or even his need for privacy among close neighbors, and so the relationship worked at a higher level.

There are plenty of business relationships that work this way too. Business is a series of agreements. To do business with someone you must be able to make and honor agreements and count on them to honor their part of the agreements. That means that every business relationship you have must be proficient at Level Two at the least, and people we work closely with, like a work team, usually have to be Level Four in order to ask for help, admit mistakes, apologize, or collaborate. These are successful relationships that work the way they need to, and they do not necessarily need to be at Level Five, even if each person is capable of a relationship at that level.

In a relationship that has been successful at Levels One through Four, if you sense both reciprocity of trust and desire for a deeper relationship on the other person's part, then the relationship will naturally be successful at Level Five and should be allowed to develop over time.

CHAPTER

10

What Can Level Five Do for You?

"How do people think of you when you aren't around?" That is the question that I ask new executives in an exercise called "Brand You." Amid their new responsibilities, this workshop calls them to be attentive to their "brand" or reputation as a leader and reminds them that they can influence how people think of them. Being in a leadership role means many eyes watching, analyzing, and scrutinizing their behavior, either publicly or privately. This sets the tone and morale of their teams and contributes to their effectiveness in their role.

Brand Yourself as a Level Five Leader

Have you ever thought about your personal brand? It's like wondering what would be said about you at your funeral. I think most people want to be known as caring for others, treating others with respect and being respectable themselves, being honorable, being a person who honors their word or agreements, being strong enough to ask for guidance when needed and admit mistakes along the way, being happy for others' success and rooting on your friends, encouraging others to be successful in their goals and being happy for them, always being happy to see someone and greeting them, listening to another's point of view, overcoming fear or peer pressure, and doing what is right. These traits are universally admired. They are the traits of a leader. They require that you be committed to Level Five Maturity in your interactions with others. When you operate at Level Five in all your relationships and meet people where they are so that you can have a successful relationship with each of them, all these things can be said about you, ideally before your funeral. Acting at Level Five Maturity will build a compelling reputation of integrity, compassion, and trustworthiness that will become your personal brand.

The following standards are what your behavior toward others will look like, and what you will be capable of, if you always strive to operate at Level Five Maturity in your relationships, while being aware of, or responding to, the maturity level of those around you:

- You treat others with human dignity and respect. (Recognition and acknowledgment)

- You treat others the way you would want to be treated. (Recognition and acknowledgment, respecting the opinions of others)

- You do not create division in your teams. You drive unity. (Honoring agreements, resolving conflict)

- You do not belittle anyone's ideas. You encourage input. (Respecting the opinions of others)

- You show up on time for meetings. You respect your employees' time. (Honoring agreements)

- You do not play games with people or try to get away with things to prove your power. (Recognition and acknowledgment)

- You are not a difficult person who disagrees or causes trouble on purpose. (Sharing facts, respecting the opinions of others)

- You honor your commitments, even to your subordinates, with integrity and always do what you said you would do. (Honoring agreements)

- You can hold people accountable and address when someone else breaks an agreement without damaging the relationship. (Honoring agreements, Broken Agreement Script)

- You can admit when you are wrong and apologize when appropriate. (Admitting mistakes, being vulnerable)

- You can accept apologies from others without holding it over their heads. (Admitting mistakes and apologizing)

- You can accept constructive and respectful correction or criticism of your work without your ego lashing out. (Being vulnerable, admitting a weakness, accepting corrective feedback)

- You can ask for help when you need it. (Being vulnerable, admitting a weakness, accepting collaboration)

- You can identify the negativity bias in your own thoughts and shift your focus so that you concentrate on the strengths of your employees, your colleagues, your friends, and your family members, so that you can help them be successful in their relationships and their work. (Being vulnerable, the negativity bias, strengths and weaknesses)

- You can give and receive positive and corrective feedback while maintaining respect. (Being less than perfect, positive and corrective feedback, intrinsic and extrinsic motivators)

- You can be trusted not to exploit the needs of others. (Intrinsic and extrinsic motivators)

- You do not talk behind someone's back. (Honoring agreements, caring for the needs of others)

- You can identify what your own needs are in a situation and express them when it is safe and beneficial to do so, therefore having a better chance of getting your needs met. (Intrinsic and extrinsic motivators)

- You can retain good employees by having a needs-based conversation. (Intrinsic and extrinsic motivators)

- You can identify why certain relationships work better for you than others, why you continue to work where you do, or why you should leave, how a personal relationship could

improve or progress, how to manage a difficult relationship in your life, how to get what you need from your most
important relationships, and how to meet the other person's
needs. (All five levels)

- You can make decisions based on objective data and what
  yields the best outcome for everyone involved, rather than
  on jealousy, power, fear, retaliation, or ego. (All five levels)

- You can identify when your ego is interfering with your judgment, your relationships, your behavior toward others, and
  thereby learn to control it with humility and self-control.
  (All five levels)

Why Do You Feel Threatened?

Let's address that last one. You read about the ego in Part 1 of
this book and how it can get in the way of building good relationships. If you have developed Level Five Maturity and can
maintain your relationships without your ego getting in the
way, then you exhibit excellent self-control over the sometimes
instinctual tendencies of the ego. It doesn't mean your ego is
nonexistent. While reading through the levels, you have probably thought about a particularly difficult person or two in your
life and then had the thought that all of this is much easier said
than done in real life when tempers flare, or when someone
offends you in some way. That is because your ego is always alive
and well, and must be monitored, controlled, and directed with
maturity when necessary. If you feel your ego getting riled up
in a situation, be sure to reflect on it later and try to honestly
identify why you felt competitive with that person, or why you
felt threatened, jealous, or offended. If that person is a sociopath
and the perceived attack was unwarranted, then your ego would
most likely not have been threatened in the first place. The fact

that you are threatened by someone or something could mean that there is an area of your life in which you feel inadequate, or it is not where you want it to be, and you could work toward improvement in that area.

For example, if I am threatened by someone bragging about their money or success, then it could mean that I either need to work on my own success because I am not where I feel that I could be, or I need to remind myself of the other things that I have prioritized in life over money and career success, and therefore calm my ego. If I am threatened by someone who is in better health or physical fitness than I am, then I probably need to make more time and commitment to improving my own health and fitness, or else be content with where I am and be satisfied with what I have traded that time for in my own life.

Here are some examples:

- Martina is a nice woman and a successful salesperson who is telling her friend Lori about her vacation last week. Lori's ego is threatened because she can't afford a vacation right now. She has been saving for a house for over a year. But she is also a mature person, so instead of feeling jealous of Martina or silently accusing Martina of bragging, Lori reminds herself of her own priorities and her own choices and realizes that she should not begrudge Martina her well-deserved vacation.

- Ronald is physically fit and spends a lot of time working out and doing outdoor activities on the weekends. Ed is caring for a sick parent at home and has minimal time to spend on fitness right now. Nonetheless, Ed's ego is threatened when Ronald is around. But Ed is a mature person so instead of feeling jealous of Ronald or pointing out Ronald's faults (negativity bias), Ed should recognize that his ego is telling him something and he may need a break for his own mental health in order to prevent burnout and resentment. He could try to carve out some time to work out on the weekends and be content with his priorities right now, reminding himself of the importance of what he is doing for his family and that the time and energy he is sacrificing along the way is worth it.

A Leader Doesn't Try to Win in a Relationship

The standards listed here are just a few of the ways that you can benefit from Level Five Maturity. Anytime you deal with people, whether it's a customer service rep on the phone, a client or vendor in your business, a colleague, a classmate, or an acquaintance at a social event, you will probably find that they are more willing to help you or get to know you better, and your interaction will be easier and more successful, if you treat them with respect and a spirit of collaboration. If you approach them with a spirit of competition, trying to win the conversation, you have eliminated the possible positive outcomes of the interaction, and are left with one possible perceived winner, and one who knows they have both lost.

Even in sales there does not have to be a winner and a loser. The notorious scenario of a seller and buyer being competing opponents is not only erroneous and outdated, but also ineffective. When I'm teaching sales skills, I address many of the techniques that give sales a bad name. If I am selling something that you need or want, I don't have to be your opponent. I am here to help you obtain a product or solution that will benefit you in some way. If I am selling something that you do not need or want, the conversation should end before we waste each other's time. There are plenty of skills a salesperson should use, and questions they should ask, in order to identify a potential client, to qualify a sales opportunity, and to quantify the value of the product or solution they are selling in order to have success in sales and be a good resource to their clients. Competition should never be a part of it. When I make a sale, it has to be a win for both my client and for me. Otherwise, the relationship will never work. There is no room for competition between my client and me, and no room for ego. If a client has been through negotiation training and approaches the sale that way, there are skills I use and questions I ask to defuse that mindset and help them see me as a potential partner in their business. This ensures there is not a winner and loser in the relationship.

Someone who can consistently control their ego and act with maturity in their interactions with other people is a leader, regardless of their title or role in their organization. Isn't that who you want in charge of your business? Isn't that who you want as a partner in a relationship? Someone who can claim success with all of these standards would be someone you could trust to act in your best interest. In my opinion, they would be a good friend, a good manager, a good parent, a good neighbor, and a good leader.

The Best Criteria for Promotions

Throughout my 30-year career I have seen some ill-advised patterns in how most businesses handle in-house promotions into management positions. The following two are the most common.

Promoting the Best Worker in the Department to Be the Manager of the Department

The most successful worker in the department is often promoted to manage the people in that department. The idea is that they should be able to teach everyone else how to do the job as well as they did. This creates problems in the organization.

You have established that if someone does the job better than anyone else then they get to be the manager of that position. Once they assume the management role, they know that if a subordinate worker on their team excels at their position, then they are poised to steal the management job. The most important responsibility of their role is to help their employees succeed at their jobs so that the company can thrive and grow under their leadership. That person is supposed to use Level Four Maturity and be good enough at giving feedback so that they raise the performance of everyone in the department to their level of expertise, so they will perform as well as they themselves did in the job. That is the goal that the company had when they promoted the best worker. The company wants everyone to be as good at the job as that person is and the assumption is that that person will lead their team to their level of proficiency at the job. However, I have seen people in this position get very territorial and endeavor to make everyone who works under them look incompetent in a paranoid effort to be indispensable, so they can secure their position with the company in perpetuity. They do not want anyone under them to be better at the job than they were, because then that worker would be eligible for the manager's job.

This attitude prevents the manager from delegating appropriately because they don't want to give a worker an opportunity to shine. I have often seen them participate in gossip about an individual who has a lot of potential. I have seen managers give incomplete or confusing instructions for tasks in order to make employees look incompetent. I have even seen a manager sabotage the career of an up-and-coming young person in their department out of jealousy and paranoia.

Where is the customer in all of this? The manager certainly cannot be focused on delighting the customer if they are preoccupied with keeping their staff in check. Who else loses here? The company loses because the department is not focused on keeping their customers happy. The workers lose because they are stifled, they cannot do their best work, they do not have an opportunity for career development, and they feel frustration instead of fulfillment. The manager ultimately loses because the productivity of the department will suffer, and they will have to do a lot of the work alone to compensate in order to hit their numbers.

Not every excellent worker who gets promoted will act this way, but this method of promotion exposes the company to this situation, and I have seen it play out this way many times.

For example, Jack is a friend who works in sales for one of my client organizations. He was the top salesperson in his department for his first two years with the company. He is talented and charismatic. Just prior to the close of his second year finishing at the top of the department, his manager restructured the accounts so that he would not be in charge of some profitable clients, many of which he had brought in and grown himself through solid sales skills and partnering with his clients to provide value-added services. Jack said there was no valid reason to restructure except to limit his success. He knew the manager was jealous of him. The manager divided up several of Jack's accounts and gave them to less productive salespeople, quoting nothing other than "fairness" to everyone in the department.

Having spent my entire career in sales, I can tell you that this is not how sales accounts are supposed to work. The result was that instead of receiving the bonus that he had earned through his hard work and expertise, he received a bonus based on a much leaner book of business. The official year-end numbers that the manager took to the board of directors showed that everyone in the department was doing a roughly equal job of generating revenue for the company, when in fact Jack was responsible for a lot of it. No one stood out as a superstar. Jack found out that there was a management position opening up and it was quite obvious that his manager did not want Jack to be promoted and be his equal in the company, fearing that Jack would quickly surpass him on the company ladder.

Jack was beyond frustrated. The last time we spoke he was considering legal action against the company, and he was actively looking for a new job.

Promoting Whoever Has Been in the Department the Longest

The idea is that the employee who has been there the longest *should be* the manager of the department. They are "up next" for promotion. There is some validity to this strategy, which is why it is still used so widely. This person has been loyal to the company, they know the company history and culture, they know the mission, vision, values, and goals. The problem with this strategy is that where the company has been is not where it is going. Staying in one place and remaining stagnant is not an option if you want to compete in a dynamic market where technology drives change constantly. A leader must simultaneously look forward 5 or 10 years to where they want to take the business, and also keep their eye on what is possible to accomplish tomorrow and next week. In this environment of trying to stay ahead of trends, the background of "I've been here a really long time" is not as powerful as it sounds. While it has value, longevity alone does not make someone the best candidate for a management position.

There is a valid suspicion that the company will lose this valuable employee if they are not promoted. They are expecting a promotion since they know that's how the company works. However, fear of disappointing this employee does not make a business case for promoting them. While losing an employee and having to replace them is a quantifiable problem, missing out on promoting the best employee to be a leader is more difficult to quantify since it involves unattained metrics, which will be never be realized without the right person leading the organization forward.

If you are trying to quantify the situation, you also have to consider how many more people will leave the company if the wrong person is put in a management role and that person is not a good manager or does not lead the company forward with measurable progress, because leaders set the standard of behavior for their employees and also set company culture.

> If a culture of immaturity, gossip, backstabbing, and petty arguments is allowed to develop, it will eventually seep into every interaction, creating mistrust, an unpleasant work environment, and roadblocks to progress until your best employees leave.

Use the Five Levels of Maturity Instead

Leaders must create a standard of behavior based on respect and teamwork that will allow their organization to focus on the customer, rather than on who is in the cubicle next to them.

In addition to the standards of behavior listed in this section, someone who can interact with others at Level Five realizes they can learn from others, even from those who do not rank as highly in the company as they do. They ask questions when they do not know the answer to something, and they apologize when they make mistakes. They delegate based on strengths and resources, not on power and politics. They encourage collaboration, brainstorming, and teamwork. They create harmony in the team by making sure that all broken agreements are addressed.

If the leaders in your organization cannot leverage that level of maturity, then their teams will suffer. Level Five is where you ignite trust, engagement, and enthusiasm in a relationship or on a team. Relationships at work are the most powerful determining factor that drives engagement and forms the culture of the organization and the team. Employees who report having a Level Five relationship with their leader are more engaged in their work, and they are willing to come in early, stay late, help others, and go above and beyond to excel in their role. The organization profits from that discretionary effort from each employee.

> Using the Five Levels of Maturity as the barometer for leadership readiness tells us when someone is capable of creating those relationships and building that confidence and trust that will be so valuable to the organization.

When you are hiring or promoting, look for someone who has Level Five Maturity because the skills that go with it are the most valuable skills in corporate America. A leader who can get the people around them to give more creativity and effort to their jobs because of their relationship is exponentially increasing their value to the organization. Either someone can come to work, do their job, and go home, or they can come to work and do their job and empower the people around them all do their jobs better because that person is there. That is the value difference.

Forming healthy relationships that add fulfillment and happiness to our lives has immeasurable value. Treating people with the respect and dignity they deserve as human beings has immeasurable value. The reason to do that is not for corporate profit. However, if you revisit the first page of Chapter 1, you will be reminded that *not* doing this costs companies money every day. In addition to the financial costs of employee conflict, people experience anguish and anxiety at work every day due to conflict with colleagues, feeling undervalued, and being disrespected. Leading relationships with Level Five Maturity is a big part of the solution to internal conflict and employee turnover. Using the Five Levels of Maturity as criteria for hiring and promoting builds an organization with respectful and mature, customer-focused teams.

Succession Planning

Fear of disappointing someone who is expecting a promotion, or the risk of promoting someone who does not have the skills to be successful in a management role, should be addressed long before a role becomes available and needs to be filled. The leaders of the company should have recognized that person's potential and should have been developing them for a promotion to make sure they have the necessary skills if they want to keep them around. Give them someone to manage in a controlled setting, give them some decisions to make to get them comfortable, and mentor them on developing their management style.

Succession planning is one of the most important leadership activities a company can pursue. People who are Level Five know how they got there. They can recognize the skills that are lacking in people they want to develop as the next generation of leaders. If the people on your frontline are not operating at Level Five Maturity on their teams, then you need to provide the coaching and mentoring necessary to get them there. Develop your people on an emerging leadership track. Create a leadership academy that teaches people how to resolve conflicts with their colleagues and how to address broken agreements with people at any level in the organization. If the people who are already in leadership positions in your company do not have these skills, then they need training on how to develop them as well, because they cannot be effective in a management or executive role if they can't get their team to honor their agreements.

Companies that don't plan for leadership succession are missing a big opportunity to make their next generation successful. If it was not worth the company's time and resources to invest in a person before a management role became available, then what they are saying is that the company will be okay without them if that person decides to leave. What they really dread is the awkward conversation when that employee resigns, and the task and expense of replacing them with someone new afterwards.

This is why forward-thinking larger companies provide benefits like professional development and even tuition reimbursement for their employees who qualify. They want to retain the employees who will pursue the skills necessary to take the company into the future.

Level Five Leadership Embraces Change

As customers decide where to spend their money, they consider the amount of time your product or solution will save for them and the quality and value that it provides. The more availability you have to increase the time you save for your customer, improve the quality you offer to your customer, and therefore increase the value you offer to your customer, the more you are leading your business forward and meeting your customer's needs. Relationship problems get in the way of companies spending more time on the most valuable activities in the business, which are continuously improving the speed and quality of services that you provide to your customer. If you can fill your organization with people who exhibit Level Five Maturity in all their interactions with others, you can minimize or eliminate these problems and work on continuously getting better and faster as a team. If you are not doing this on a regular basis, if you are staying stagnant, then you are mismanaging your business and exposing it to becoming irrelevant and fading away in the near future.

Even an established business must continuously improve if they want to continue to delight their customers and stay in business. For any organization to be relevant, it must continuously adapt and improve by embracing recent technologies, a customer base that shifts with generational influences, and current cultural trends. If things are going to improve, they cannot stay the way they are. Change is inherent in the process of improvement, but there is a natural human resistance to change.

Some people are survival-minded, and they do not want to rock the boat. Their instinct is "Hey, what we've done up until now worked because we are still alive today, so don't change anything!"

Some people resist change because it's difficult. Their instinct is "I'm used to the way I do things now; I can whistle while I work, and I don't have to think too hard about my processes." If things change, they have to think about what they're doing, focus, be present, and think through every task until they master the new process. That is uncomfortable and exhausting. The bottom line is that some people are too lazy to embrace that, or they don't feel it's worth it to put in that extra effort in exchange for the same salary. In other words, to put it bluntly, "Why should I work harder? What's in it for me?"

Some people resist change because it threatens their ego. Their instinct is "I don't want to look stupid because I don't know what I'm doing. I'm really good at my job now, and if things change, then I'll be a rookie at these tasks like everyone else." In my workshops, I ask people to sign their name on a paper, then switch hands and sign it again with their nondominant hand. This is obviously so uncomfortable because they are doing something unfamiliar, and the results will not be as good. You cannot do something at an expert level when you are doing it for the first time. You don't look smart or competent until you've had experience with it and had a chance to learn it and master it. Agreeing to that takes humility and commitment to a common goal of improvement.

As a leader, if you are going to ask an employee to overcome their resistance to change, to overcome their survival instincts, their comfort zone, and their ego, you need their buy-in. Employees who do not want to cooperate with change will cause a new initiative to fail, or to be overbudget in time and costs, and to underperform its goals.

What will drive their decision to cooperate with the latest changes and embrace an attitude of continuous improvement? The number-one factor will be their relationship with the leadership of the company, and with their direct manager. If they have witnessed executive wars, previously abandoned initiatives and agreements, refusal to apologize, dismissing others' opinions, and a "my way or the highway" attitude, then your idea for improvement will not have a lot of credibility with them, and your lofty initiatives will not be a reason for them to put forth extra effort. They might assume the idea has not been road-tested or collaborated on and given feedback. If your ego is in charge, then they won't trust your motives, and they won't be willing to cooperate and change their comfortable job just to placate your whims and increase your profits. If enough employees feel this way, there will be a lot of employee gossip, resentment, and pushback. However, if your leadership style is to ask for feedback, collaborate and use teamwork, admit mistakes and learn from them, and ask for expert guidance, and if they trust that you are a Level Five leader who has the best interests of the company in mind, and you know the real boss is the customer and that's all that matters, then they will know that your idea is the best chance of benefiting the company and its stakeholders, including them. It is worth their time and discomfort and learning curve to cooperate and help make it successful.

Your employees have to trust that you are a team player, that you will listen to others on the team, and that you value serving the customer over your own ego. The way to gain that trust is to lead your relationships with all the skills presented in the Five Levels of Maturity. If they know that you have their own needs and best interests in mind, they also know that you have the customers' best interests in mind and that your leadership is focused on moving the business forward. That's the way to get better and faster as a team and focus on delighting the customer into the future to ensure that the business will thrive in the dynamic environment of today's business markets.

Incorporate These Concepts into All Your Relationships

Relationships work on the same premise regardless of whether they take place in a business environment or in a personal environment. They work when both people get their needs met. When the ego and competition sneak in and you seek to satisfy your ego by winning against the other person, then you can no longer meet each other's needs, and the relationship will not work. If you seek continuous improvement in your own life, then you won't be tempted to get your identity from sizing up against the people around you, and then you won't feel competitive against others. You can actually root for them to be happy and productive and successful in all of their efforts. This allows you to navigate your relationships through the lens of the Five Levels of Maturity and form healthy relationships, which are the cornerstone of a fulfilling life.

Controlling the ego and eliminating competition in relationships is a lifelong pursuit. I hope you have great success with it, just not more than I do. Just kidding – it's not a competition.

The Concentric Circles of Leadership Model

Three Vital, Learnable, and Teachable
Leadership Skills

– By Steve McClatchy,
Alleer Keynotes & Workshops

Leadership is a choice you make, and in every situation, there is an opportunity to lead. Anyone, in any situation, can be a leader. Instead of being a title that you hold, leadership is a result you produce by making something better than it was before. In every situation, and in every endeavor, you are either alone, with another person, or with a group. The three concentric circles of leadership build on each other and demonstrate why we should lead and how we should lead in each of these situations: personal leadership, leading relationships, and team leadership. They work together to help us overcome the challenges that business leaders face. As a business leader, do you have proficiency in all three circles? If your answer is no, the good news is that these skills are learnable. Developing these skills throughout your organization will have an immediate impact on your company's culture and success.

Personal Leadership is leading, or improving, yourself by setting and pursuing goals that will improve your life and make tomorrow better than today. Before you can lead others effectively, you must lead yourself on a path toward continuous improvement. Working on personal goals keeps you excited about your life and your future. When you don't create excitement in your life for an extended period of time, burnout sets in. It is your job to keep yourself from getting burned out. You need to manage all that is expected of you efficiently and effectively enough so that you still have capacity to pursue goals like learning new skills, building new relationships, and experiencing new things.

Pursuing continuous improvement in your life, instead of just the daily maintenance of life, will prevent you from comparing and feeling competitive with others, especially the people you are supposed to be leading. No one wants to work for a leader who competes against them. Your team needs you to *help* them succeed, and you can't do that if you are burned out and resentful of their energy and accomplishments. Great leaders only compete against their own personal best, not against others. Pursuing continuous improvement and leading your life forward, not just managing it, builds positive self-identity and self-esteem, which is the foundation of personal leadership, and which is necessary to build healthy relationships with others. My book *Decide* is a deep dive into this topic.

Leading Relationships is developing, nurturing, and supporting functional, respectful relationships among business colleagues, managers, and employees so that we can build trust and confidence in the people around us, stop competing with each other, and focus on serving the needs of our customers.

As a leader, you need to get a team of people to work together harmoniously and maximize the best talents and abilities in each one of them. The two most valuable skills you will need to do this are delivering feedback that improves the performance of others, and holding others accountable for their agreements in a way that doesn't damage the relationship.

We all have strengths and weaknesses. A leader needs to know how to work around the weaknesses and highlight and leverage the strengths of their people. When a weakness cannot be worked around, a leader needs to be able to mentor and give feedback in a way that improves the weakness until it is manageable.

A leader needs to address conflict and hold people accountable for their agreements, not only in their own relationships, but also between team members. You need to consistently set clear expectations and make agreements about the work that needs to be done and the values of the organization that must be upheld, including treating each other with respect. You must also hold others accountable for these expectations and agreements, and facilitate one-on-one relationships that are free from competition, games, ego battles, and immaturity. With these relationship issues out of the way, you can focus on getting better and faster as a team so that you can keep your focus on the customer. My book *Leading Relationships* is a deep dive into this topic.

Business Leadership is improving your quality and speed to serve the customer better. Once burnout and competition among colleagues is off the table, and as a cohesive team you are ready to move your business forward, you can work on the systems and processes that run your business. The more time you can spend in this category as a leader, the more you can increase profits and increase your ability to achieve your company mission and purpose. If you can build a company culture of respect, support, innovation, collaboration, and engagement, get relationships where they need to be so that everyone can work together successfully, and keep your teams focused on the customer, then you can turn your attention toward leading your business forward.

Your job as the leader of a team is to work *on*, not just *in*, your systems, processes, workflow, and structure so that your team continuously gets better and faster at delivering a quality work product to its customers, whether they are internal or external customers. Your customers expect and deserve that focus, and it's the job of your team to deliver on that expectation every day.

Leadership is continuous, never-ending improvement, which means you never arrive, and you are never finished with leadership. It means that you always have work to do, to make things *better*. This requires welcoming and evaluating every idea based on its merit of improving quality and speed, regardless of who it came from. It requires acknowledging and celebrating progress along the way. It requires a lot of experimenting, brainstorming, collaborating, and willingness to fail and to learn. Your customer needs your team to deliver the best-quality solutions for their business. If you always put those needs first, then it will be obvious that there is no place for burnout, resentment, complacency, internal competition, or conflict in your team.

Today's business leaders need competency in all three of these concentric circles of leadership. These skills are teachable, learnable, and vital to the success and growth of your business. If you recognize that a leader in your business has these skills, then take the time to thank them today, because they are moving your business forward and contributing to its strong future.

If you have interest in developing these skills within your organization, email me at Steve@Alleer.com and we can set up a time to discuss how I might be a resource to you and your business.

The Dos and Don'ts of the Five Levels of Maturity

THE DOS & DON'TS OF THE FIVE LEVELS OF MATURITY

LEVEL OF MATURITY	DO	DON'T
1 RECOGNIZING & ACKNOWLEDGING PEOPLE	ALWAYS BE POLITE. ACKNOWLEDGE PEOPLE YOU KNOW AND RESPOND TO COMMUNICATION.	DON'T GIVE THE SILENT TREATMENT! DON'T PLAY GAMES OF POWER & PUNISHMENT.
2 EXCHANGING FACTS & HONORING AGREEMENTS	BE AGREEABLE. DO WHAT YOU SAY YOU'RE GOING TO DO.	DON'T BE A DIFFICULT PERSON!
3 NAVIGATING DIFFERING OPINIONS	RESPECT OTHERS. BUILD A BUSINESS CASE FOR DIFFERING OPINIONS.	DON'T BE A BULLY!
4 PLAYING TO STRENGTHS & WORKING AROUND WEAKNESSES:	CONCENTRATE ON STRENGTHS, WORK AROUND WEAKNESSES, ADMIT MISTAKES, APOLOGIZE, PROVIDE EFFECTIVE FEEDBACK.	DON'T CRITICIZE OTHERS TO GET AHEAD. DON'T WITHHOLD POSITIVE FEEDBACK.
5 UNDERSTANDING INTRINSIC & EXTRINSIC MOTIVATORS	WORK IN MY BEST INTEREST.	DON'T TAKE ADVANTAGE OF ME OR EXPLOIT WHAT YOU KNOW ABOUT ME.

Notes

Part 1

1. State of the American Workplace Report, Gallup, 2017, https://www
.gallup.com/workplace/238085/state-american-workplace-report-
2017.aspx

Chapter 1

1. J.E. Dutton and B.R. Ragins (Eds.), Exploring Positive Relationships at
Work (Mahwah, NJ: Lawrence Erlbaum Associates, 2007).
2. Shane McFeely and Ben Wigert, "This Fixable Problem Costs U.S.
Businesses $1 Trillion," Gallup, March 13, 2019, https://www.gallup
.com/workplace/247391/fixable-problem-costs-businesses-trillion.aspx
3. B.B. Lamberth, Workplace bullying in healthcare: part 3 *Radiology
Management* 2015;37(3):18–22; quiz 24–25. PMID: 26314175.
4. L. Mäkelä, J. Tanskanen, and H. De Cieri, "Do relationships matter?
Investigating the link between supervisor and subordinate dedication
and cynicism via the quality of leader–member exchange," *Journal
of Leadership & Organizational Studies* 28, no. 1 (2020) 76–90, 10.1177/
1548051820967010

    Employee Job Satisfaction and Engagement: The Road to Economic
Recovery, accessed March 29, 2024, https://3311812.fs1.hubspotuser
content-na1.net/hubfs/3311812/Resources/14-0028%20JobSatEngage_
Report_FULL_FNL.pdf

    Dorothea Wahyu Ariani, "Relationship with supervisor and co-workers,
psychological condition and employee engagement in the workplace,"
Journal of Business and Management 4, no. 3, 34–37, https://www
.researchgate.net/publication/283619173_Relationship_with_Supervisor_
and_Co-Workers_Psychological_Condition_and_Employee_Engagement_
in_the_Workplace

5. Gary Namie, "2021 WBI U.S. Workplace Bullying Survey," accessed January 16, 2024, https://workplacebullying.org/wp-content/uploads/2024/01/2021-Full-Report.pdf

6. James Campbell Quick and Demetria Henderson, "Occupational stress: Preventing suffering, enhancing wellbeing," *International Journal of Environmental Research and Public Health* 13, no. 459, (2016), 10.3390/ijerph13050459

7. Naomi I. Eisenberger, Matthew D. Lieberman, and Kipling D. Williams, "Does rejection hurt? An fMRI study of social exclusion," *Science* 302, 290–292 (2003), 10.1126/science.1089134

8. K. Uvnas-Moberg and M. Petersson, "Oxytocin, a mediator of anti-stress, well-being, social interaction, growth, and healing," *Zeitschrift für Psychosomatische Medizin und Psychotherapie* 51, no. 1, (2005) 57–80 (German), 10.13109/zptm.2005.51.1.57. PMID: 15834840

9. Naomi I. Eisenberger, Matthew D. Lieberman, and Kipling D. Williams, "Does rejection hurt? An fMRI study of social exclusion," *Science* 302 (2003): 290–292, 10.1126/science.1089134

Chapter 2

1. "Revenge in the Workplace," Insurance Quotes, accessed May 13, 2024, https://www.insurancequotes.com/business/revenge-in-the-workplace.

Chapter 7

1. "U.S. Vehicle-Miles," Bureau of Transportation Statistics, accessed April 12, 2024, https://www.bts.gov/content/us-vehicle-miles

Chapter 9

1. John Bevere, The Bait of Satan (Lake Mary, FL: Charisma House, 2014); *used by permission.*

Acknowledgments

Thank you to Alicia Simons for your marketing expertise, patience, and assistance in getting this project off the ground. Your contributions enhanced this project immensely, and I always learned from our conversations. I am lucky to work with such an expert in the publishing field, and also to call you a friend.

Thank you to our team at John Wiley & Sons: Shannon Vargo, Cheryl Segura, Amanda Pyne, Michelle Hacker, and Kim Wimpsett. You brought us into the Wiley family and made us feel comfortable since our beginning days with *Decide*. Thank you for your enthusiasm around this project and for your dedication to making this book the best that it could be.

Thank you to Tara Kaufman for being my right arm, my business copilot, and my cherished friend. Thank you for shining your light on Alleer and on my family. I hope we have many more wonderful years of working together!

Thank you to Scott Ulrich and David Hartmann of D2S Designs, once again, for your artistic talent and vision in turning our thoughts into pictures. I continue to be impressed by your ability to decipher stick-figure art.

Thank you to my mom, Kay, and my mother-in-law, Jackie, for your support and prayers. Lynn and I are very blessed to have you both as examples of unconditional love.

Thank you to my family and friends for your support and encouragement during this process. I could not have finished this project if I didn't have fun events with all of you to look forward to along the way.

Finally, and most importantly, thank you to my wife, Lynn, and to our children, Grace, Amy, Kyle, and Kelly, for giving me so much to work for. I love you beyond words.

About the Author

Steve McClatchy is an international keynote speaker, entrepreneur, and author of the award-winning *New York Times* bestseller *Decide: Work Smarter, Reduce Your Stress, and Lead by Example*, which has enjoyed global success and has been translated into 11 languages.

Steve has delighted thousands of audiences with his entertaining style and powerful stories. Into every keynote speech and workshop, he weaves insight, interaction, and actionable content with humor, inspiration, and motivation. Steve has worked with many of the most prominent business and sports organizations in the world as well as small and midsize companies with equal relevance and impact. He has been quoted in the most prestigious print media, has appeared on national business news programs, and is a regular lecturer in several of America's top business schools.

Steve grew up in the greater Philadelphia area as the 11th of 12 children in his family. He has been in the professional development industry since 1996. He has been part of the Big Brother program since 1987 and has been a lifelong Big Brother to

Max Mitchell. A portion of the profits from this book are donated to the Big Brothers Big Sisters of America. Steve and his wife are the dedicated parents of four hilarious young adults and are just trying to get everybody through college.

Learn more at www.alleer.com.

Index

Page numbers followed by *f* refer to figures respectively.

benefits of operating at, 204–206
branding yourself as a leader
at, 203–206
and embracing change,
216–219
failure at, 181, 195–198
high stakes of, 181–182
imperative nature of, 182–184
quick reference guide for, 185
success criteria for, 175
and whys and wants of our
choices, 176–181
Unhappy, being, 38, 39, 106
Unresolved problems, 88
Upper hand, trying to gain the, 48,
83, 101–102

Value:
and competition, 116
creating, for customers, 1

Values, organizational/company,
82, 85
Verbal agreements, 86
Vulnerability, showing, 65

Weaknesses, working around,
134, 136–143
"Whys and wants" of our
choices, 176–181
Wi-Fi networks, 86
Win-lose situations:
avoiding, 208–209
focus on winning in, 36, 40–41
games as, 47
Withholding:
of positive feedback, 146–148
of recognition and
acknowledgment, 59, 63–65, 79
Working environment, pleasant, 19
Written agreements, 86